Game of My Life
Memorable Stories of Razorback Football

Rick Schaeffer
Foreword by J. Frank Broyles

SP
SPORTS
PUBLISHING
L.L.C.

www.SportsPublishingLLC.com

ISBN: 1-58261-988-3
© 2005 by Rick Schaeffer

All photos provided by the University of Arkansas/Collegiate Images.

Publishers: Peter L. Bannon and Joseph J. Bannon Sr.
Senior managing editor: Susan M. Moyer
Acquisitions editor: John Humenik
Developmental editor: Elisa Bock Laird
Art director: K. Jeffrey Higgerson
Cover/dust jacket design: Dustin Hubbart
Interior layout: Heidi Norsen
Imaging: Dustin Hubbart, Heidi Norsen, and Kenneth O'Brien
Photo editor: Erin Linden-Levy
Vice president of sales and marketing: Kevin King
Media and promotions managers: Jonathan Patterson (regional),
    Randy Fouts (national), Maurey Williamson (print)

Printed in the United States of America

Sports Publishing L.L.C.
804 North Neil Street
Champaign, IL 61820

Phone: 1-877-424-2665
Fax: 217-363-2073
Web site: www.SportsPublishingLLC.com

Contents

Foreword

J. Frank Broyles
Director of Athletics
University of Arkansas

The Razorbacks are an extended family that spreads beyond our own borders into nearly every area of the country. When Razorback fans gather, they remember the good times, just as families do. They remember the details of games played long ago just as if those games had been played yesterday. Memories connect Razorback athletes and fans with a bond that lasts a lifetime.

Game of My Life captures many of those memories by sharing the stories of Razorback heroes who have entertained and thrilled us over the last 50 years. I had the privilege of coaching many of the players featured in this book and am reminded of what a wonderful time it was for all of us when they represented the Razorbacks.

More than just the games, the personalities of some of the greatest players in Razorback history are revealed in this volume. Constant themes that appear in these chapters are the love these Razorback athletes have for their teammates as well as the gratitude and deep affection they express for the University of Arkansas.

You will enjoy these glimpses of the lives of Razorback greats.

Acknowledgments

As a voracious reader but first-time author, I have come to realize how much cooperation it takes to write a book. This project was made possible by the gift of time graciously extended by each of the Razorbacks represented in this volume.

The 24 players featured are just the tip of the iceberg among the vast number of legends who have worn the Razorback jersey. If this book had twice as many chapters, it would not cover the spectrum of all of the great players who have created such wonderful memories for all of us who love the hog on the helmet.

Special thanks to Arkansas athletic director Frank Broyles, whose trust allowed me to spend 24 great years working in the Razorback athletic department; to Kevin Trainor and Mary Lynn Gibson in the sports information office, whose cooperation proved immeasurably valuable; and to John Humenik, the former sports information director at Florida, whose friendship I treasure and who contacted me about this and future projects.

And greatest thanks to Adelaide, my wife of 22 years, whose encouragement allowed me to finish this book when so many other things could have taken higher priority. Other than Jesus, she is God's greatest gift to me, and I will never be able to adequately express my love for her.

One-third of the author's net proceeds from this book will be donated to Champions For Kids, a nonprofit organization whose primary purpose is to partner with agencies that perform a multitude of services for Arkansas youth.

CHAPTER 1

JASON ALLEN

Born: February 23, 1972
Hometown: Edmond, Oklahoma
Current Residence: Springdale
Occupation: Director of Sales, Leggett and Platt Aluminum Group
Position: Quarterback
Height: 6-0
Weight: 190
Accomplishments: Passed for 1,152 yards and eight touchdowns during his career; was the starting quarterback in 1991, the Razorbacks' final season in the Southwest Conference, until suffering a knee injury in Arkansas's seventh game; started the first half of 1992, the Hogs' first year in the Southeastern Conference.
The Game: Arkansas vs. Texas, October 19, 1991, Little Rock, Arkansas

BACKGROUND

Jason Allen's football career started very early.

"My family has pictures of me throwing a football in my uncle's yard when I was three years old," Allen explains. "My dad grew up in Duncan, Oklahoma, where football is very big, so he's always loved the game.

"I was playing tackle football when I was seven years old. I was a center for two years and then moved to quarterback. I had four cousins who were all older than me, and we played football all the time. So I played with kids four to six years older than I was. My cousins pushed me. They had a big influence.

"Dad coached me in Little League. He played football at Central State in Edmond. We were in Duncan when I was young and I watched Quinn Grovey score 50 touchdowns for his seventh grade team. Each year we would go back to Duncan at times, and I followed Quinn's career. I knew a lot about him long before he knew who I was."

Rick Jones was his high school coach at Edmond. Allen calls him the kind of disciplinarian who would push you.

"He was single at the time and he breathed football," Allen recalls. "He's taken teams to four state championship games, including 2004 at Greenwood Arkansas where he coaches now, but we were his first.

"My junior year we were 10-0 in the regular season but lost our second playoff game. My senior season we started 1-2 but won 11 in a row and earned the first state championship in school history. Edmond hasn't won one since. They've split into three schools now. A couple of them have made it to the title game but have never won."

When his senior season had been completed, Allen had few college choices. Only a late coaching change at Arkansas enabled him to receive a scholarship from the Razorbacks.

"I didn't even know where Fayetteville was," Allen says. "I knew nothing about Arkansas' history or tradition. Growing up in Edmond, Oklahoma and Oklahoma State were all we heard about.

"Jim Donnan had been an assistant at Oklahoma before getting the head-coaching job at Marshall. He was the first coach to offer me a scholarship. OU, OSU, and Tulsa either had quarterbacks or were recruiting quarterbacks they thought were better than I was. So I committed to Marshall."

The week Allen committed to Marshall he got a surprise visit from Charlie Weatherbie, who had just been hired to coach quarterbacks at Arkansas. Weatherbie convinced Allen to at least visit the UA campus.

"Arkansas had changed coaches and had not signed a quarterback," Allen recalls. "I was impressed on my visit. Fayetteville was only three and a half hours from Edmond. Marshall was a 17-hour drive. Jack Crowe, the new coach, told me I reminded him of a quarterback he'd coached at Clemson who wasn't flashy but got his team in the right play and won games. He offered me a scholarship. I called Coach Donnan to tell him I was going to Arkansas."

Allen redshirted in 1990, Quinn Grovey's senior year and third as the Razorbacks' starting quarterback. Just before fall drills opened in 1990, Arkansas announced it was leaving the Southwest Conference for the Southeastern Conference. A newly arrived freshman, Allen didn't know what to think.

"I didn't grow up in Arkansas, so I didn't think much about leaving the Southwest Conference," Allen says. "I thought of the SEC as a great opportunity. It wasn't emotional for me at all. In fact, when I had looked at the 1991 schedule figuring that would be the first season I would have an opportunity to play, I was motivated by playing Miami at Little Rock. That was a game I really wanted to play in.

"During the season I carried charts and kept some statistics on the sidelines. I was a freshman, trying to learn the system, and we were losing. Arkansas had been to two straight Cotton Bowl games. I was stunned by our poor season. I was also surprised by how hostile the crowds were. Those Southwest Conference fans hated us for leaving the league. It was a tough year all around."

THE SEASON

Grovey had graduated, and the Hogs were coming off a 3-8 campaign, their first losing season since 1967. Allen, a redshirt freshman, competed with Gary Adams for the starting job during the spring.

"Gary got hurt during a scrimmage, and I took the first offense down the field to a touchdown," Allen explains. "From that point on, I was the starter."

However, two weeks before the season opener Allen broke his hand in practice.

"I had fumbled, and Coach Crowe told me to dive on the ball," Allen says. "I came down on my hand. It was a freak thing. It kept me out for four weeks."

Allen's dream of playing against Miami didn't come true. He returned in the third game of the year. He led the Hogs to a narrow victory over Southwestern Louisiana and then quarterbacked the Razorbacks in a close loss to Ole Miss. Arkansas was 2-2 and set to open its final SWC season.

"We went to Fort Worth and were down 21-0 in the second quarter," he remembers. "TCU had beaten us 54-26 the year before in Little Rock. That game in Fort Worth is one of my best memories. It taught us that if you don't give up and play as a team, good things happen.

"Our defense had a great mentality, and our offense came a long way that night. I remember throwing a pass to Ron Dickerson and what a great catch he made. That led to a score. We came back to win 22-21 and that was the night things started to jell for us. That game gave us the feeling we would have a successful season."

The following week the Razorbacks met Houston at Fayetteville. The Cougars' run-and-shoot offense had embarrassed the Hogs a year earlier in the Astrodome. Houston had been still throwing deep passes at the end of a 62-28 thrashing of the Razorbacks.

"We were a much more confident team after beating TCU, and we were able to beat Houston 29-17," Allen recalls. "That was sweet after what they had done to us the previous season."

THE SCENE

When Arkansas had announced its departure from the SWC, a league it had belonged to since 1914, the Razorbacks became the target for hostile attitudes from the other eight league members, all located in Texas. The possibility of Arkansas winning the league title horrified the other SWC schools. When the Hogs entertained Texas at Little Rock, it might have been the only time every league member but Arkansas pulled for the Longhorns to win a conference game.

"We were pumped to play Texas," Allen says. "I was a young, dumb freshman. After we beat Houston I was thinking, 'Bring on the world.' But I was also a little scared. My dad had taken me to six or seven Oklahoma–Texas games, and I was passionate about wanting to beat Texas. I remember watching Peter Gardere lead Texas to a win over OU, and he was the quarterback we would be facing at Little Rock.

"We put some new wrinkles in our offense, and I was engrossed in trying to learn my part. We could feel the atmosphere on campus. It was tense, like we were at war. Students and teachers kind of left us alone. They realized we were under pressure and didn't want to bother us.

"We didn't change our practice routine, but everything we did was elevated. Every practice had a degree of intensity that other weeks didn't have. Adrenaline came at an unsurpassed level.

"When we arrived at the stadium the crowd was already unbelievably loud. It was an early kickoff, and the weather was awesome. I had missed the Miami game, so this was my first time to play at Little Rock. I was in a zone from the time we walked on the field. It all happened so fast."

THE GAME
by Jason Allen

I didn't realize Texas was so big until our first offensive series. When our offensive line bent down, there they were. Texas was intimidating. Their players have always looked great in their uniforms. Texas recruits the best of the best.

Jason Allen

I had to settle myself down. We had some pass plays early that were real close, but we didn't quite connect. We thought our game plan was very good. We wanted to keep them off balance. We knew we would need some breaks to win. We needed something good to happen to boost our confidence.

They fumbled to give us the ball on their end of the field. Against Houston the week before we had run a play action sweep fake and then threw a screen pass. Because Texas was so aggressive in their secondary, we baited them by faking that screen pass. The cornerback sucked in, and Dickerson broke past him.

The play requires a unique pass. It's a touch pass, but it also has to get there on time. When the play was called, I was excited. We had practiced it all week, and we knew it would work. I saw Ron break open. He made the catch and outran the safety to the end zone. It was a 30-yard touchdown. When he scored, the crowd was so loud. It was a surreal moment. It was great to score first.

In the second quarter we used an option play to score. We wanted to slow Texas's aggressiveness by giving them some different option looks. Reading their defensive end was the key. He was playing wide, giving me an easy read. I rode Kerwin Price into the line and left the ball in his belly. The line blocked well, and he busted loose up the gut and ran 18 yards for a touchdown.

We were feeling it then. For an offense that wasn't among the league leaders, we were having some success. At halftime the coaches told us to keep doing what we had been doing. Field position would dictate our play calling. Coach Crowe, knowing he had a freshman at quarterback, got more conservative.

Texas made some adjustments, and we couldn't capitalize on anything. I missed some throws, and we kept going three and out. If we had third and six, we'd make five yards. If we had third and eight, we'd make six or seven. It put a lot of pressure on our defense to stop them.

It was frustrating, because we knew it would come down to a last drive. We thought we would have to make a big play on offense. They were stopping our running game.

Texas scored a touchdown in the third quarter and another one early in the fourth. They were kicking the extra point to tie the game and missed. Did we get a break there! Once they missed, I thought if we could control the ball and get a field goal, we would win. Todd Wright was our kicker, and he was exceptional.

Texas stopped everything, though. The longer we played, the harder it became to make first downs. Our offense just couldn't get it done. But Texas's kicker became our best friend. They moved the ball down the field and had a chance to win with a field goal. They tried a 39-yard field goal, but he pushed it. Once he missed, we believed we would win. There wasn't much time left.

They didn't get close enough to try another field goal. I'll never forget taking a knee on the last play of the game. It was great seeing the smiles on our players' faces. Mark Henry was our leader. He hadn't played on a team that beat Texas. Seeing him and the other guys made it all worthwhile.

There was a great celebration in the locker room, but at the same time I was frustrated because our offense didn't do its job in the second half. Coach Crowe told me we would get that fixed, and I should enjoy the moment.

Then we went back into the stadium to salute our fans. No one had left. Besides winning the national championship, I don't know how anything could feel better than that win over Texas. After the 1990 season, our program really needed something positive. My younger brother, Jared, found me on the field, and I put him on my shoulders. That picture was in the paper the next day. He later became a quarterback at Florida Atlantic, and he could carry me on his shoulders these days.

POSTGAME

Arkansas had an open date the following week, giving Hog fans two weeks to celebrate a victory in their last ever SWC game against Texas.

"It was great," Allen says. "We wanted to go to practice. We loved going to class. I went to the OU–Kansas game that weekend. Knowing how OU feels about Texas, it felt great going to that game knowing we had defeated Texas the week before. Also, it was great knowing I had quarterbacked in a win over Texas because I hadn't been good enough for OU to recruit me."

Allen and the Hogs came back to reality the next week. On a frozen field in Fayetteville, the Razorbacks lost a 9-5 decision to Baylor. They also lost Allen for the season.

"I had an uneasy feeling before that game," Allen recalls. "A player never thinks about getting hurt, but on the way to the game I wondered what would we do at quarterback if something happened to me. Gary Adams had moved to defense, and our only other quarterback was Wade Hill, a walk-on who was redshirting.

"Baylor was good, and our offense was just starting to move the ball in the third quarter. I picked up a first down on an option when my knee buckled. It was a hard pill to swallow. Our offense was improving. I still believe we would have won the league title that year if the injury hadn't happened."

The Hogs finished 6-6. Allen rehabbed but probably rushed his return in order to start the 1992 opener. It led to the low point of his career.

"I could feel my ability was diminished," he says. "I should have rehabbed for 12 to 18 months but came back in 10. I didn't get my knee all the way back until my senior year.

"I started against The Citadel, and we lost. We took them for granted. We only had one deep pass in our game plan that week. The next day Coach Crowe was fired. We were in a state of disbelief. It was tough getting ready each week. We were on a roller coaster the rest of the year.

"The coaches decided to replace me with Barry Lunney, a freshman, the week we played Tennessee. It hurt, but it was the right thing for the team. We needed a playmaker at quarterback, and I wasn't making plays. It proved to be a coming-out party for Barry."

The Razorbacks upset Tennessee but finished 3-7-1. Danny Ford was named head coach. Allen did some soul searching, wondering what his role would be.

"God was trying to get me to understand my identity wasn't just as a football player," Allen says. "I was here for another purpose. I became determined to learn how to fulfill my role and finish strong. I wanted to be a good example to my teammates, coaches, and our fans."

After the 1993 season he thought about transferring to Missouri Southern, where he might have been the starting quarterback as a senior.

"I was all but packed to go, but the Lord impressed on me to stay and be a leader," Allen explains. "It worked out well. Barry and I became great friends, and the team voted me a captain for the 1994 season. I held for kicks and even played some at wide receiver. I met my wife, Michelle, that year, and we got married in January of 1995."

WHAT HAPPENED TO JASON ALLEN?

After graduating Allen worked two years for the Fellowship of Christian Athletes and then worked briefly as a youth pastor in Kansas City. But he and his wife missed northwest Arkansas. They moved back, and he went to work with Pace Industries and has been with the company, now called Leggett and Platt Aluminum Group, since. He and Michelle have a daughter, Olivia, seven, and a son Grant, five.

"Looking back, my experience as a Razorback was wonderful. I quarterbacked the last Southwest Conference victory over Texas and the school's first SEC win at South Carolina. Those were days I will never forget."

CHAPTER 2

GARY ANDERSON

Born: April 18, 1961
Hometown: Columbia, Missouri
Current Residence: Little Rock
Occupation: Private Business
Position: Tailback
Height: 6-1
Weight: 180
Years Lettered: 1979-1982
Accomplishments: Was the only Razorback ever to be named Most Valuable Player of three bowl games—the 1980 Hall of Fame Bowl, the 1981 Gator Bowl, and the 1982 Bluebonnet Bowl; was All-Southwest Conference in 1982; rushed for 1,999 career yards and owns the UA record for most all-purpose yards with 4,435; scored 19 career touchdowns; holds the school record for punt returns with 115 and had 1,004 return yards, second best ever at Arkansas.
The Game: Arkansas vs. Florida, December 31, 1982, Bluebonnet Bowl, Houston, Texas

BACKGROUND

Gary Anderson always liked football, but as a youngster growing up in Bearden, Arkansas, he played strictly basketball when he wasn't helping out his grandparents who took care of him.

"I grew up playing in the neighborhood," he recalls. "But I liked basketball best. I was strictly a basketball player in school until the ninth grade.

"During that time in Arkansas my grandfather owned a barber shop," Anderson recalls. "I helped in their garden. I was just getting by."

His affinity for basketball continued even after he left Bearden to live with his mother in Columbia, Missouri, after he finished the fourth grade.

It wasn't until he was in ninth grade that he tried football—even though the attempt was short lived. After breaking a team rule, Anderson was kicked off the football team and forced to focus on the other sports he was involved in— basketball and track.

Once he moved up to high school, the football coach convinced him to try the sport again.

"On the first day the coach told me where to go and to beat the other guy there," Anderson recalls. "I did that. They put me at running back, and I was a starter by my second game."

He was never dislodged, and by the time he was a senior he was a coveted recruiting prize.

"Missouri recruited me hard," he says. "We lived in Columbia, and my mom worked at the school. But my grandparents were in Arkansas, and I figured if I went there and had any trouble, I could get to them quickly."

However, his first contact with an Arkansas coach almost turned into a nightmare.

"Jesse Branch was recruiting me for Arkansas," he says. "I had never met him. He came to my house, but I was out with Kelvin Winslow on my visit to Missouri. My mom visited with Coach Branch for a while and then went to bed. Coach Branch waited for me in the living room but fell asleep on our couch.

"When I came home and found a man sleeping on our couch, I went to get a baseball bat. I was going to hit him. He jumped up, told me who he was, and told me not to hit him. We hit it off from there. We've laughed about that visit many times since then."

Anderson hadn't been too familiar with the Razorback program until the Hogs upset Oklahoma in the Orange Bowl a year earlier following the 1977 season. During the recruiting process he took a close look at the Razorback roster.

"Ben Cowins, Micheal Forrest, and Donny Bobo were seniors and would be gone by my freshman season. Roland Sales, the hero of the Orange Bowl, would be a senior. My high school had played against Ben's team for the state championship when I was in junior high, so I knew of him.

"When Lou Holtz visited, I told him all I wanted was a fair opportunity to play. He told me he would give me that. I wanted to get out on my own, so I chose Arkansas.

"When I first got there I wanted to be a defensive back. I was looking forward to that. Coach Holtz wanted to see me on offense. After I had two 70-yard runs in practice, I stayed on offense."

Anderson was part of one of the best incoming classes in UA history. Included were Billy Ray Smith, Richard Richardson, Darryl Bowles, Kim Dameron, and Ron Matheney, all of whom joined Anderson as starters by early in the 1979 season. Several other freshmen played, and by the end of 1982 the group had won 34 games with two bowl victories.

"Thomas Brown and James Tolbert were there with Sales at running back," Anderson says. "Coach Holtz liked straight-ahead runners. I liked to bounce outside then cut back. Coach Holtz gave me flak until he figured out what I was doing. I had to prove I could get outside, then go north and south. Once I did, he was fine."

Anderson scored his first touchdown against Texas in the Hogs' 17-14 win at Little Rock.

"George Stewart and Robert Farrell threw great blocks on the play," Anderson recalls. "It was a thrill to get the first touchdown against Texas."

The Razorbacks finished 10-1, sharing the Southwest Conference title with Houston. The Hogs lost to eventual national champion Alabama in the Sugar Bowl, but the loss didn't dampen Anderson's year.

"It was a great year," he says. "Our class already was becoming close. It was a class like no other."

Some quality seniors had had a major impact on the success of 1979, and in 1980 the Hogs found themselves struggling.

"We had a lot of the same guys, but we weren't winning like the year before," Anderson explains. "It was frustrating for Coach Holtz. We would have great practices but came up short on the field.

"We really needed to finish strong, and we did by beating Tulane in the Hall of Fame Bowl. We jumped in front and stayed on them."

Anderson had an 80-yard punt return for a touchdown in that game.

"I thought they had me boxed in, but I sidestepped a tackler and went down the sideline," he recalls. "There were some great blocks on that play."

The next season looked to be a difficult one, because the competition in the conference was stiff.

"SMU had Eric Dickerson and Craig James," Anderson remembers. "Baylor, Texas, and Houston were very good. It seemed like every opponent was in the top 10."

Still, the Hogs won eight games and played North Carolina in the Gator Bowl, a contest played in thick fog.

"I hated for them to punt," Anderson says. "You couldn't see the ball. Everyone was in the same boat. North Carolina had a great team. They beat us but not by much. Brad Taylor made some great throws in the fog."

THE SEASON

With so many seniors back, the 1982 Razorbacks made every preseason top 10. The Hogs won their first seven games with only one close call, a 14-12 victory over Ole Miss.

"We wanted to leave a good impression," Anderson says. "This was our last time together. We wanted to go to the Cotton Bowl. Arkansas hadn't been in a while. We had great coaches and great players, and we were motivated to do well."

In the eighth game the Hogs were upset at Baylor. They bounced back with a win over Texas A&M to set up a showdown with undefeated SMU for a spot in the Cotton Bowl. The Razorbacks had to win and then beat Texas to earn the Cotton Bowl's host spot.

More than 25,000 Razorback fans helped fill Texas Stadium in the SWC's game of the year.

"We played very well," Anderson recalls. "We gave it everything we had. In the end, it was a tie. SMU scored its last touchdown after a terrible pass interference call. We knew we had been the better team, but that call really hurt. We were devastated. It was like losing, since it ended our chances at the Cotton Bowl."

Emotionally spent, the Razorbacks lost their regular-season finale at Texas and then got ready for their first ever matchup with Florida in the Bluebonnet Bowl.

THE SCENE

The Bluebonnet Bowl gave the senior players the opportunity to turn the disappointment of not making it to the Cotton Bowl into a triumphant last stand.

"We knew the Bluebonnet Bowl would be the last time our senior group would play together," Anderson says. "We were disappointed with the end of the regular season but wanted to go out with a win.

"All we heard about was Wilbur Marshall and the great Gator defense. No one was giving us a chance. None of us wanted to leave on a losing note.

"Our coaches had us very prepared. We knew Florida was good, but we thought we were better."

THE GAME
by Gary Anderson

We got off to a great start. Our offensive line was really good with guys like Steve Korte, Jay Bequette, and Alfred Mohammed. We moved the ball on them right away, and we took the early lead.

I scored a touchdown on a 16-yard run right up the middle. The blocking was really good. I cut to the left and scored. I remember diving into the end zone because I saw two defensive backs coming. I dove in before they could hit me.

After that we had a tough time moving the ball. They kept us pinned up in our own territory. They had three long drives for two touchdowns and a field goal, and by halftime we were down 17-7.

At halftime I remember thinking about how good their defense was. Tim Newton, their nose guard, was giving us a hard time. But our offensive line made adjustments and did a great job of blocking in the second half.

We knew we would need some long drives against them, because we never had very good field position. We also needed to keep the ball away from their offense. Twice we had to overcome 10-point deficits.

We knew we couldn't just run against them, and Brad Taylor hit some big passes in the second half to keep our offense moving. In the third quarter we had an 83-yard drive, and I dove over from the one-yard line. It was a fourth-down play, and it wasn't easy.

They scored to go back ahead by 10, but we had two great drives in the fourth quarter. Tom Jones threw a short touchdown pass to Jessie Clark to end the first drive, and Tom ran a quarterback sneak for the go-ahead score.

Our defense really stepped up in the fourth quarter to give us a chance. By then we knew we could move the ball. We were in the I Formation all night. When we got the ball back with the lead, we ran outside to run the clock and keep the ball out of their hands. I think our last drive went over 80 yards, and we ended the game inside their 10-yard line. We used nearly seven minutes on that drive. We never gave them a chance to get the ball back.

I rushed for 161 yards and they named me MVP, but the entire team deserved it. We had stuck together for four years. Everyone was an MVP.

There was nothing like playing with our group for four years. Playing pro football was a dream, but that last game with our senior class was something I will always remember.

Gary Anderson

WHAT HAPPENED TO GARY ANDERSON?

Following the Bluebonnet Bowl Anderson prepared for the NFL draft. "We had a lot of players who would be drafted," he recalls. "After the game we all had to fend for ourselves. You always wonder if you will ever see your teammates again once you leave campus."

In the spring of 1983 the United States Football League had been established as a rival to the NFL. Anderson was the fifth player picked by the New Jersey Generals in the USFL draft and was the 20th player selected by the San Diego Chargers in the NFL.

"I had the same agent as Herschel Walker," Anderson remembers. "They thought it was more important for Herschel to play in the big market, so they put him in New Jersey and sent me to Tampa Bay."

Anderson played for coach Steve Spurrier and thoroughly enjoyed his three years in Tampa before the league folded.

"We had great ownership," Anderson remembers. "The owner took the linemen to dinner every week, because he knew they weren't the glamour players, but they were so important to the team."

San Diego still owned Anderson's rights so he became a Charger in 1986. He played there four years.

"Don Coryeal was our coach," he explains. "He spread the ball around. We had some great receivers, like Kelvin Winslow, Charlie Joyner, and Wes Chandler. It was a fun offense. I made it to the pro bowl while I was there."

After sitting out a year because of a contract dispute, Anderson went back to Tampa Bay and spent three seasons with the Buccaneers. He played for the Detroit Lions for a year before his NFL career ended.

He wasn't finished with football, though. He played a year for the Memphis Mad Dogs of the Canadian Football League and could have gone back for more but decided against it.

"I wanted to be with my family in Little Rock," he says. "I still wanted to play. I was just in my 30s. But I realized it was time to get on with my life."

After working a year and a half for the postal service, he joined the Arena League Arkansas Twisters as an assistant coach. After a year he was named head coach and remained in that position for five years.

"I enjoyed it more than a regular job," Anderson says. "I loved helping young players with their careers. I wanted to help them get to a higher level. I even ran routes with them. My playing time may be over, but I still did conditioning with them. It was fun. I'd like to coach again."

Anderson and his wife, Ollie, have five children. Akia is 25 and lives in Missouri. Antisha is a senior and runs track at Ole Miss. Gary Jr. plays football and runs track at Rice. Anderson has two younger daughters, Adeeja and Asia, still at home in Little Rock.

CHAPTER 3

DeCORI BIRMINGHAM

Born: November 22, 1982
Hometown: Atlanta, Texas
Current Residence: Boston, Massachusetts
Occupation: Pro Football, New England Patriots
Position: Tailback-Wide Receiver
Height: 5-11
Weight: 200
Years Lettered: 2001-2004
Accomplishments: Rushed for 1,151 career yards; caught 57 passes for 592 yards; had 546 yards in punt returns; set a school record for career kickoff return yards with 1,321.
Game: Arkansas vs. LSU, November 29, 2002, at Little Rock, Arkansas

BACKGROUND

DeCori Birmingham knew about Arkansas long before the Razorbacks knew about him. His cousin, Randy Garner, was a standout defensive lineman for the Hogs, and Birmingham followed Garner's career closely while playing high school football in Atlanta, Texas, also Garner's hometown.

"I remember watching Clint Stoerner, Anthony Lucas, and Chrys Chukwuma," Birmingham says. "I was excited about the Razorbacks. When Randy went there, I was hooked.

"Still, I looked at Texas as well as Arkansas. Randy called me before Arkansas and Texas played each other in the 2000 Cotton Bowl. When Arkansas won the game, it built their program up. At the time I didn't understand the Arkansas–Texas rivalry. I just knew my interest in Arkansas was sparked even higher."

Texas remained relentless in recruiting, but finally Birmingham firmly committed to the Razorbacks.

"Coach Mack Brown was great, but so were coach [Houston] Nutt and his staff," he explains. "There are so many schools in Texas but just one in Arkansas. The Razorbacks are like the NFL team of the state. It's a big family with great fans and support."

Birmingham didn't grow up calling the Hogs, but he grew to love football at an early age.

"My father and grandfather both played football," Birmingham says. "My father played college ball at Arkansas–Monticello. I was too young to understand what was going on then, but I remember being in the locker room and seeing everyone after my dad's team won.

"I've always enjoyed football. It takes away everyday stress. When I was 10 years old, I played for a team called the Cowboys. We lost our first game but didn't lose again. I figured out quickly I didn't like losing. I was a quarterback then, because I was the most athletic member of our team."

He played junior high football in Texarkana, Arkansas, where he moved from quarterback to tailback. He remained a running back throughout his junior high and high school career. Plenty of colleges were interested in him, but only Arkansas and Texas kept his attention.

Once he decided on Arkansas, he knew his chances for playing early were good. In 2001 the Hogs used him at tailback and receiver, and on kick returns. His most memorable moment came in one of the most historic games in Razorback history, the seven-overtime victory at Ole Miss.

"The Ole Miss game was unreal," Birmingham says. "One overtime is exciting. I never thought seven overtimes would happen. I kept thinking if we found a way to stop them, we would win. It was like a tug of war. It just kept going and going."

The game was tied 50-50 going into the seventh overtime. After the Hogs scored a touchdown, Birmingham caught a two-point conversion pass from

Matt Jones that proved to be the difference when the Rebels failed on their two-point try after producing a touchdown. Arkansas won 58-56.

"I wasn't supposed to get the ball on the two-point play," Birmingham recalls. "Matt was scrambling, and I thought he would run. Then he threw it up, and I came down with it. I was his third or fourth option as a receiver."

Arkansas finished strong and met Oklahoma in the Cotton Bowl.

"They were the defending national champions and beat us 10-3," Birmingham recalls. "That game told us we could play with anyone and gave us high hopes for the following year.

"That was my first collegiate experience. I never thought of it as a learning experience. They threw me into the fire as soon as I got to Arkansas. It was exciting. I thought I could make something happen."

THE SEASON

Birmingham had been positioned at wide receiver to start the 2002 season. He spent the summer working with returning veteran George Wilson and looked forward to a good year.

"I knew the kind of team we could have," Birmingham says. "Matt was a great quarterback, and our offensive line made things happen. We won our first two games but lost to Alabama and then lost in six overtimes to Tennessee.

"The next week we won at Auburn. We felt if we could keep it going, we could end up being very good. I had no idea we would play in the SEC championship game, though. We started winning, and that set up a showdown with LSU."

With Birmingham playing a key role, the Hogs followed a loss to Kentucky with wins over Ole Miss, Troy State, South Carolina, Louisiana–Lafayette, and Mississippi State. Arkansas carried an 8-3 record into its season finale against LSU in Little Rock.

THE SCENE

With Alabama ineligible for the SEC title, Arkansas and LSU played in Little Rock to determine the Western Division's representative in the SEC championship game. At that time the Razorbacks were 13-0 at Little Rock under Nutt's direction.

"Coach Nutt talked to us about never losing at Little Rock," Birmingham says. "That was real important to us. We didn't want to snap that streak of always winning at War Memorial Stadium.

"As a team, LSU was awesome. They were very gifted. When you play someone like that, you can't be afraid of them. We respected them but thought we were just as good.

"There was added pressure with the winner going to the SEC championship game, but Coach Nutt never harped on that during the week. He just wanted us to play our best."

THE GAME
by DeCori Birmingham

LSU hit us with some big plays early. They kicked a field goal on the last play of the half to go ahead 10-0. Even though we hadn't done much on offense, we knew we were still in it.

LSU was really good on defense, but we thought we could make corrections and come back. Our team never gave up. That was a trademark of Arkansas's football team that year. We never gave up. We believed in the saying that it's not over until it's over.

We scored a touchdown pretty early in the third quarter to make it 10-7. We had a nice drive and thought we could continue to move the ball in the second half. But LSU scored again, and we were down 10 points again going into the fourth quarter.

We got back in the game on a long touchdown run by Fred Talley. He ran 56 yards for the touchdown. There was a little over six minutes left when that happened. Without that run we would have been looking for answers.

Fred told me he was going to make something happen. He sure did that. He made two or three of their tacklers miss him on that run and then with his speed he went all the way. That was a huge play in the game. That touchdown made what happened at the end of the game possible.

We couldn't wait to get the ball back, but LSU drove down the field and ate up almost all the time. They kicked a field goal to make it 20-14. If they would have scored a touchdown, the game would have been over, but our defense held when it had to.

There were only 40 seconds left when we got the ball back. We were at our own 19. All day we wide receivers had asked Coach Nutt to give us a shot, because we believed we were better than LSU's defensive backs.

We hadn't thrown much up to that point but really didn't have a choice. There wasn't much time left.

The first play was designed for Richard Smith. He was supposed to go 20 yards, catch the ball, and get out of bounds. But the cover guy slipped, and Richard was wide open for a 50-yard gain. When he made that catch, we knew we had a chance.

Another reason we had a chance was our offensive line. They were tired. They had played the whole game against that great LSU defense. On that last drive, though, they did the dirty work. After that completion to Richard, those linemen sprinted down the field. They knew how little

DeCori Birmingham

time was left, and they knew we had to set up in a hurry. Everyone knew we had one more play in us.

On first down we threw an incompletion, but that stopped the clock and gave us time in the huddle. The play was designed for George Wilson. He was to go 15 yards and go out of bounds after catching it. I was supposed to be a decoy. In fact, if George was covered, the next two options were Richard Smith and Sparky Hamilton.

I ran to the end zone to take the safety away from the other receivers. I saw Matt scrambling, and I saw him throw the ball up. When I watched the play later, I could see there were two defenders right there, but while I was focusing on the ball, I didn't even see them.

I was in the back of the end zone and happened to jump at just the right time. After I caught the ball and came down, I was afraid I might be out of the end zone. Thank goodness I wasn't. I saw the referee signal touchdown, and the next thing I knew everyone was jumping on top of me.

As a kid you dream about catching the game-winning touchdown on the last play of the game, but I never imagined that would happen to me. We were penalized 15 yards for celebrating, but even the coaches had a hard time blaming anyone. When you score a touchdown like that near the end of the game, you shouldn't be surprised if half the players on the bench come running on the field.

So we had scored the touchdown, but the game wasn't over. David Carlton still had to make the extra point, and it was more like a field goal because of the penalty. When he made it, we celebrated again, but this time not on the field. With nine seconds left we knew we had the game won.

It was unbelievable in our dressing room. We had won the Western Division championship. The way we won was like something you see on TV, but it doesn't happen to you. There were a lot of tears and a lot of hugs in there. From the end of the 2001 season, that's what we had worked for. All that work had been worth it.

POSTGAME

Houston Nutt thought the win over LSU so exhausted his team that the Hogs weren't recovered by the time they played Georgia in the SEC championship game. The Bulldogs defeated the Razorbacks in what Birmingham called "an overwhelming experience."

"The Georgia Dome was full of Georgia fans," he says. "We had great fans there, but we were very outnumbered.

"Still, beating LSU earned championship rings for our team. It was a moment we will always treasure."

Birmingham still had two years of eligibility. He opened the 2003 season as a receiver, and the Razorbacks roared to a 4-0 start with road wins at Texas and Alabama. Losses to Auburn and Florida slowed Arkansas's momentum, but later that year Birmingham had the opportunity to experience another historical game.

"I moved to running back since Cedric Cobbs and De'Arrius Howard were injured," Birmingham says. "When we went to Kentucky, it was the first time in my college career I was the premier running back."

Birmingham never dreamed the Hogs could play another seven-overtime game, but they did. That's how long it took for the Razorbacks to defeat the Wildcats 71-63. Birmingham carried 40 times for 196 yards and raced 25 yards for the winning touchdown on the first play of the seventh overtime.

"The Kentucky game was much different than the Ole Miss game for me," Birmingham says. "I was much more involved. I did a couple things against Ole Miss but played a bigger role against Kentucky.

"I scored my first touchdown of the season in the first quarter and ended up carrying the ball 40 times. On the touchdown in the seventh overtime, I will never forget seeing Matt Jones downfield blocking for me. When the defense stopped them after we scored that last touchdown, we all had a feeling of elation."

Arkansas won its ninth game that season in the Independence Bowl, whipping Missouri 27-14. Even with Cobbs back and earning 141 yards, Birmingham had 10 carries for 85 yards.

The 2004 season wasn't as enjoyable for Birmingham, because the Razorbacks finished 5-6. However, Jones was the only returning starter on offense that year, and the Hogs suffered through plenty of growing pains as the season progressed.

"It was fun to watch our team grow," Birmingham says. "We would have liked to have gone to a bowl game, but I saw a lot of guys grow up that year. Our offensive line went from being thrown into the fire to jelling as a unit. I was elected one of the captains and considered it an honor to give direction to our younger players."

Birmingham realizes his legend will grow with time.

"Wherever I am recognized, people ask me how I caught that ball against LSU. I don't mind. I can talk about it all day. It was a great memory. I have so many great memories of my career at Arkansas."

WHAT HAPPENED TO DECORI BIRMINGHAM?

Signed as a free agent with New England in the spring of 2005, Birmingham hopes to spend time in the NFL but is also preparing for a career in real estate.

"I love football," he says. "It's still a little boys' game, just like it was when we were young and played with a balled-up sock instead of a football. But I know it will end sometime. When football ends, I will miss playing, but I look forward to selling real estate. I want to work in northwest Arkansas so I can still hear people call the Hogs."

CHAPTER 4

SCOTT BULL

Born: June 8, 1953
Hometown: Jonesboro
Current Residence: Fayetteville
Occupation: Vice President, Leggett and Platt Aluminum Group
Position: Quarterback
Height: 6-5
Weight: 209
Years Lettered: 1973, 1974-1975
Accomplishments: Was 14-1 as a starting quarterback during his career but was best remembered for leading the Razorbacks to victories over second-ranked Texas A&M and then Georgia in the Cotton Bowl in the final two games of the 1975 season; produced 448 total yards and seven touchdowns during the final half of the 1975 campaign.
Game: Arkansas vs. Texas A&M, December 6, 1975, Little Rock, Arkansas

BACKGROUND

Scott Bull played football in his backyard since he knew what a football was. He and his older brother, Claud, played one on one, with his father filming everything with his Bell and Howell.

"Claud was bigger than me, but I was faster," Bull says. "I would signal for him to come at me. He would, and I would dart around him every time. We've still got the old films."

Bull's first organized football experience was a YMCA program when he was in the fourth grade in Greenville, Mississippi. He became a quarterback in the sixth grade. Once after a game he remembers telling his dad he forgot that people could tackle him during the game because of his scrambling ability.

"I asked him to remind me," Bull explains. "I always believed I could score on every play if I was determined. I was hard to tackle."

As the years went along, Claud got faster and Scott got bigger. They moved to Blytheville and played a year of junior high football there before moving to Jonesboro. Claud played quarterback as did Scott. Don Riggs, Jonesboro's coach, depended mostly on a running attack but decided his team would be more wide open during Scott's junior year.

"In our first game Claud threw 23 passes and completed two," Bull recalls. "Our wide receivers dropped five or six passes. I played tailback and scored the only touchdown. We won 10-0. Coach Riggs changed the offense the next week. He put me at quarterback and Claud at tailback. We played No. 1-ranked West Memphis and beat them 7-0 with Claud running for 120 yards.

"We ran right at people and threw it some. About halfway through the year we figured out I needed glasses. Coach Riggs would signal the play in from the sideline and even squinting I had a hard time seeing. Claud would tell me the play, and I would call it in the huddle. I got glasses the next week, and we started passing a little more. We made it to the championship game before losing to Springdale."

As a senior Bull directed Jonesboro back to the state title game, and he played despite a shoulder separation. Against Hot Springs, Bull had one of the worst moments of his career.

"We were winning 9-7 and moving the ball," Bull says. "I ran the option and had a clear path to the end zone. The ball went behind my back and fell to the ground. It was one of those moments that was frozen in time. I turned around but just couldn't get the ball. Hot Springs recovered and came back to beat us 14-9. I felt terrible for my teammates, some of whom never got the opportunity to play football after high school."

Even though he played high school football in Jonesboro, Bull had always wanted to be a Razorback. His dad grew up just outside Pine Bluff and had been a Hog fan his entire life.

"When we lived in Greensville, we would get in Dad's car to listen to the Razorback games on KAAY. We couldn't get it in the house. That's where we were listening when Jon Brittenum took the Razorbacks down the field for the winning touchdown in the 1965 Texas game. I was a very big Hog fan."

He was also a very good baseball pitcher. He had offers to sign out of high school, but Coach Riggs talked him out of it.

"He encouraged me to get a college education," Bull says. "So I had to decide between Arkansas, Arkansas State, Vanderbilt, and Tulane.

"Bennie Ellender was the coach at Arkansas State. He had played the previous quarterback for four years, and they were unbeaten one of those seasons. He said I would be his quarterback and would start for four years. Freshmen could play at that level during that time but not at division one. I was considering it, but Coach Ellender left for Tulane.

"He tried to get me to come to Tulane, and I liked Vanderbilt, too, but I couldn't get past wanting to wear a helmet with a hog on it. I was a big fan of Bill Montgomery, and he was just completing his career at Arkansas. After I chose Arkansas, Coach Riggs gave me the best advice I could have received. He told me to keep going no matter how tough it got."

It got real tough during the spring of his freshman year. He had played quarterback, tight end, strong safety, and defensive end for the freshman team in 1971 but wanted to be a quarterback for the Razorbacks. When he was asked to move to tight end, he nearly left Fayetteville.

"I was listed last on the depth chart at tight end, and my first thought was about going home," Bull says. "Coach Riggs told me to stay. He told me I wasn't a quitter. At the same time I was moved to tight end, I was pitching for the baseball team. I loved baseball, but coach [Frank] Broyles made it clear that I needed to participate in spring practice if I hoped to play the next year. I went back to football and didn't play baseball again until my senior year.

"Joe Ferguson was our quarterback going into the 1972 season. Mark Miller and John Booty, a hot recruit from Louisiana, were behind him. But during the spring Miller hurt his knee, and Booty went home. The coaches asked me to spend the summer in Fayetteville working out as a quarterback.

"So I was the backup quarterback. One game early in the season our fullbacks didn't block. They had the fullbacks, tailbacks, and backup quarterbacks block defensive ends in practice for what seemed like an eternity. At the end of the drill there was just one fullback left—me.

"For two weeks I was the fullback blocking for Dickey Morton. We had some real good fullbacks in Marsh White and Mike Saint. After two weeks those guys must have got the message, because they moved me back to quarterback.

"The offense we were running had been developed by Don Breaux, but he left before the 1972 season. As defenses dropped seven and eight men into coverage, we didn't adapt very well, so the coaches made some changes.

"Against SMU in the snow, Joe and I alternated at quarterback. I handed to Morton when I was in the game. On one play I ran downfield and threw a block for him. That week in the film room Coach Broyles ran the play back over and over and was complimenting me. I was embarrassed, but the next week in practice we put in the Slot I, and I practiced as much as Joe.

"Right before our last game against Texas Tech, Coach Broyles told me I was starting. I played every play, and we won. I know it hurt Joe. It was his last game. I've always been impressed with the way he has returned and embraced the university after suffering through that disappointment.

"In the spring of 1973, I became the starting quarterback. But two weeks before our 1973 opener at Southern Cal, I hurt my knee. Mike Kirkland became the starter, and I redshirted.

"In the spring of 1974 Mike played baseball and went to last on the depth chart. Mark Miller and I battled for the starting job. In the meantime, I decided to get married on August 31, just before the season started. Coach Broyles has never told me, but I think that made him mad. Mark played the whole game against USC, and we beat them in Little Rock."

The Hogs struggled through much of the 1974 season with Bull, Kirkland, and Miller sharing time at quarterback.

"We played Colorado State in a midseason non-conference game, and we were told whoever played the best would start the rest of the year," Bull explains. "All three of us played, but I started and led us to a 21-0 lead. We won easily, and I was feeling pretty good about things.

"But, the next week I was running plays with the scout team and never played. Several of the coaches liked Kirkland because he had such a good arm. The pro passing game was a big deal then, and Mike had the best arm among us."

THE SEASON

Kirkland returned as the starter in 1975 with Bull as the backup, and Miller moved to defense. Bo Rein was hired as offensive coordinator and installed the Veer Offense.

"It was an offense made for me," Bull says. "We could have beaten anyone in the country with that offense. We had a great team."

The Hogs were 1-1 when Kirkland suffered a knee injury against Tulsa. Bull was the starter from that point on.

"We barely beat TCU during my first week as a starter, but the next week at Baylor we ran the Veer the way the Veer should be run. We ran all over them. We were very confident in the offense at that point."

Next up was the annual showdown with Texas, the game that stirs indescribable emotions in every Razorback fan and player.

"When you come to Arkansas, you want to beat Texas," Bull says. "Joe [Ferguson] led us to a win over Texas my freshman year, but our group had never beaten them. In 1975 I had an experience similar to that state championship my senior year in high school.

"We had a better team than Texas, but we made all kinds of mistakes. I threw three interceptions, and we had several fumbles. On one drive I had carried the ball four or five times in a row and was tired and numb. I should have called a timeout. The snap hit my hand, but I never felt it. The ball went to the ground.

"It was another one of those moments frozen in time. I saw the ball but couldn't get to it. Texas recovered. We lost the game by six points, and I'm sure many of the fans blamed me.

"I did get a little personal revenge. That spring I pitched against Texas and beat them at Austin with a complete game. I was the second Arkansas pitcher ever to beat Texas at Austin. Richard Miller had done it two years previously. A few years later I met Roger Clemens and told him about beating Texas. He didn't seem very impressed."

Arkansas bounced back with wins over Utah State, Rice, SMU, and Texas Tech to improve to 8-2.

"Coach Broyles and Coach Rein gave us a chance to win every game because of our offense and their halftime adjustments," Bull explains. "I think we scored on the first possession of the third quarter in just about every game that year. After the Texas game, none of our coaches or players blamed anyone. We were a team. Anyone could have been successful playing quarterback that year. The coaching was superb, and eight of our offensive starters, including all five linemen, ended up playing in the pros.

"And we had a great defense. They overachieved. We didn't have as many future pros on the defensive side. They played with determination and intelligence. And they played extremely hard. If our offense failed to move the ball, the defense would do something. I admired every one of those defensive players. They were outstanding."

THE SCENE

ABC television had moved the Arkansas–Texas game to the end of the season in 1969 and 1970. The gamble paid off big time both years. In 1975 Texas A&M had a terrific team, and ABC switched the UA–A&M game to December.

"Texas A&M was 10-0, had just beaten Texas, and was ranked second nationally," Bull remembers. "If we won, there would be a three-way tie for first [in the conference] and we would go to the Cotton Bowl. The loser was headed for the Liberty Bowl.

"Texas A&M had the best defense in the country. They had Ed Simonini and about eight other defensive players who made it to the NFL. It seemed like they had six or seven shutouts that year.

"We didn't put anything new into our game plan. We had moved the ball against everyone and thought we could make enough plays to win. We were very ready."

Scott Bull

THE GAME
by Scott Bull

After the pregame warmups the position coaches always met with their players. Bo Rein huddled the running backs and quarterbacks together in the shower of our dressing room at War Memorial Stadium. Before long the linemen joined us, then the whole defense came. We were all gathered in the shower with Coach Rein talking to us.

I don't remember a word he said, but I do remember it was the greatest pregame speech I had ever heard. He was practically foaming at the mouth as he told us what we had to do to win. I've never been so motivated by what someone said. I knew we would win.

We played every play as hard as we could play. Our defense set the tone. I don't remember Texas A&M getting a first down in the first half. Our defense gave an effort that should be used as an example for all Razorback teams.

We stuffed the fullback in their Wishbone in the first half. The entire half was a stalemate. A&M was very good on defense. They stopped us as well.

Late in the half they had a short punt to give us good field position. We made a first down and then called a pass. Teddy Barnes became "the immortal Teddy Barnes" with the catch he made to put us ahead. He caught it between two All-Americans. They jumped at the wrong time, and at the top of his jump Teddy caught it in the back of the end zone. His arms were fully extended, and he was falling backward as he made the catch.

I don't remember if I even saw him open. I threw it into the area where I thought he would be. I was just about to be hit when I let go of the ball. That play gave us a 7-0 halftime lead and set the tone for the rest of the game. Both defenses were so good that we had the feeling whoever scored first would win.

In the second half we moved the ball much better. I threw a deep pass to Doug Yoder to set up a touchdown. Freddie Douglas was in the area, too, and those guys still tease me about throwing to Freddie and Doug catching it. The whole second half couldn't have gone better. A&M scored a touchdown, but it didn't matter. We had the game under control.

Late in the game A&M fumbled deep in its own end. We recovered, and on the next play I scored on a four-yard run. I got hit with a forearm, and blood came gushing out of my nose. We were on such an emotional high I didn't even think about it.

There was a great exhilaration after the game. I remember how loud the A&M fans were before the game and how quiet they were at the end. Winning a football game isn't the greatest thing about life, but winning that game was a great experience. We had to earn it.

POSTGAME

A few weeks later the Razorbacks earned a 31-10 victory over Georgia in the Cotton Bowl after trailing 10-0.

"We were down, but the defense made two big plays near the end of the half that set up a touchdown and field goal for us," Bull recalls. "As usual, we made adjustments at halftime, and they had a hard time stopping us after that."

WHAT HAPPENED TO SCOTT BULL?

In the spring Bull pitched for the Razorbacks and wanted to sign a contract with the Red Sox. However, a St. Louis Cardinal scout told him how hard life in the minor leagues was and how difficult it was to make it to the majors, so he opted for the San Francisco 49ers who drafted him in the sixth round.

At the end of his rookie season the 49ers upset the Minnesota Vikings with Bull at the helm. On the plane home coach Monte Clark told Bull he would be the quarterback the following year. However, Clark was fired shortly thereafter, and Bull was a backup for most of his career.

After three years in the NFL he and his wife, Becky, moved back to northwest Arkansas. He went to work for Pace Industries, now Leggett and Platt Aluminum Group, in 1979. His son, John Scott, is 26 and lives in Fayetteville. His daughter, Leanne, is married to former Razorback offensive lineman Kenny Sandlin and lives in Lowell.

CHAPTER 5

RON CALCAGNI

Born: February 6, 1957
Hometown: Youngstown, Ohio
Current Residence: Conway
Occupation: Vice President for Marketing for Arkansas Sports Entertainment
Position: Quarterback
Height: 6-0
Playing Weight: 188
Years Lettered: 1975-1978
Accomplishments: Was All-Southwest Conference in 1977, leading Arkansas to 10-1 regular season; completed 50.8 percent of his career passes with .602 completion percentage in 1978, his senior season.
The Game: Arkansas vs. Oklahoma, Orange Bowl, January 2, 1978

BACKGROUND

Growing up in Youngstown, Ohio, Ron Calcagni didn't know much about University of Arkansas football. Anyone who followed the college game at that time knew about the Arkansas–Texas rivalry and coaches Frank Broyles and Darrell Royal, but for Calcagni, the Ohio State Buckeyes were the most well-known program.

After completing a brilliant high school career, Calcagni wasn't sure where he would play college football. In fact, he signed several conference letters of intent before inking a national letter with Arkansas.

What persuaded him to choose the Razorbacks? After all, Fayetteville is a long way from Youngstown.

"Bo Rein had been recruiting me at North Carolina State," Calcagni says. "That's one of the schools I signed a conference letter with. All of the sudden, Coach Rein left to join Frank Broyles's staff at Arkansas. He told me he wanted me to come with him.

"Once I visited the campus, I was very interested. Bo Busby was my host. We hit it off. He loved nature, so he showed me the hills and the beauty of Arkansas. I also thought I could play early. Arkansas had three quarterbacks who were all going to be seniors my freshman year."

Those seniors were Scott Bull, Mike Kirkland, and Mark Miller. Kirkland was hurt early in the 1975 season—Calcagni's freshman campaign—and Miller moved to defense. Bull led the Razorbacks to a 10-2 season that included a victory over Georgia in the Cotton Bowl.

Ironically for Calcagni, Rein left after the Cotton Bowl victory. He had restored life to the Razorback offense and was hired as head coach at North Carolina State. Following the 1979 season he was named head coach at Louisiana State University but tragically died in a plane crash before he ever coached a game for the Tigers.

Meanwhile, Calcagni became the starting quarterback on what turned out to be Broyles's last team as head coach. He was only the second sophomore (Bill Montgomery in 1968 was the other) ever to earn the starting quarterback job for Broyles. The Hogs were 5-1-1 and undefeated in the Southwest Conference when Calcagni was hurt against Texas A&M and knocked out for the season. The Razorbacks never recovered from the injury and lost their final four games.

Broyles stunned the collegiate football world by resigning after 19 years as head coach following the 1976 season, and Lou Holtz was hired as his replacement. This was the same Holtz who was head coach at North Carolina State when Calcagni had signed a conference letter of intent with the Wolfpack.

"Like any new coach, Coach Holtz interviewed all the players," Calcagni recalls. "He told me I didn't have a chance to play. He said I wasn't tough enough, and he resented my signing with NC State, then going to Arkansas. He was motivating me. He always knew what buttons to push.

"I went through spring practice and hurt both of my thumbs. At one point I had casts on each of my hands. But I played in the spring game to show him I was tough enough to play."

Calcagni earned the starting job that spring, holding off the charge of No. 2 signal caller Houston Nutt, who later became head coach for Arkansas.

THE SEASON

Arkansas and Texas, the longtime bullies of the Southwest Conference, were both under new coaches for the first time in two decades. They were picked middle of the pack in the league, but the 1977 season turned out just like so many others. The winner of the Arkansas–Texas game went to the Cotton Bowl, and the loser got another New Year's Day invitation.

The Razorbacks set up their showdown with Texas by running the table against New Mexico State, Oklahoma State, Tulsa, and Texas Christian University. Arkansas outscored its first four opponents 160-25.

Hog fans were ecstatic. Holtz's popularity was rising quickly. But then the hated Longhorns popped Arkansas's balloon at Fayetteville.

Texas edged the Razorbacks 13-9. Arkansas was able to hold dominant running back Earl Campbell in check most of the day, but he took a screen pass to the Razorback two-yard line in the fourth quarter to set up the game's only touchdown. Three Steve Little field goals, including an NCAA-record 67-yarder, were not enough for the Razorbacks. The Longhorns finished the regular season 11-0 and earned a spot opposite Notre Dame in the Cotton Bowl.

Arkansas didn't lose another game. The Hogs rebounded with a 34-0 victory over Houston then won easily against Rice and Baylor. Calcagni hit Robert Farrell with a late touchdown pass to earn a win at Texas A&M, and Arkansas accepted the Orange Bowl bid after thumping Southern Methodist University at Fayetteville. Hog fans showered the field with oranges. After seeing so many oranges come from the stands, Holtz said he was glad Arkansas had not been invited to the Gator Bowl.

The Razorbacks took a 9-1 record to Texas Tech for a Thanksgiving Day nationally televised regular-season finale. After so many easy wins, the Hogs were threatened at Lubbock.

"We already knew we were going to the Orange Bowl," Calcagni says, "but we wanted to win out and take a 10-1 record there. Texas Tech jumped on us early and stopped everything we did in the first half and led 14-3 at halftime. It was the only time I ever saw Coach Holtz nervous. When we went into the locker room, I told him, 'Let's run the veer and control the line of scrimmage. We can beat them.' Sure enough, that's exactly what we did. We won the game to finish 10-1."

THE SCENE

Arkansas had never played in the Orange Bowl. Razorback fans responded by buying 17,500 tickets to the game against Oklahoma, a border rival that the Hogs hadn't played in decades. Holtz had treated bowl practices like a preview of spring workouts. In their last on-campus workout, the Hogs lost All-America offensive guard Leotis Harris to a knee injury. Holtz was furious. He hated to lose such a reliable offensive lineman. However, the worst news was yet to come.

Just before Christmas Holtz suspended running backs Ben Cowins and Micheal Forrest along with wide receiver Donny Bobo for breaking team rules. Combined, those three scored 78 percent of Arkansas's regular-season touchdowns. Fans were shocked. The three players sued for reinstatement but were denied.

"Coach Holtz called me at home," Calcagni remembers. "I thought he was going to wish me a Merry Christmas. Instead he told me he had bad news. He had suspended Cowins, Forrest, and Bobo. My heart went to my belly. Then he told me we would go on without them and someone would step up.

"I came back to Fayetteville to fly on the team plane to Miami. When I visited Coach Holtz's office, he told me how we would win the game. He showed me the opening sequence for the first four plays. He told me no one would handle the ball but me for four plays. Then he told me we were going to win big.

"I found out later that while he and his coaches were working on the game plan he visited Coach Broyles in his office and asked if Arkansas could win the national championship by beating Oklahoma. Coach Broyles told him it was possible but unlikely. Then Coach Holtz asked if we could win the national championship if we beat OU decisively. Coach Broyles told him we would at least have a good chance."

No one else dreamed the Razorbacks would win, much less win big. Like Arkansas, second-ranked Oklahoma, a perennial power under Barry Switzer, had lost only to Texas. With Arkansas's three stars suspended, the game was taken off the betting line. OU already had been a two-touchdown favorite.

"When we arrived at Miami, there wasn't anyone who gave us a chance to win," Calcagni says. "We got tired of being told who wasn't there. We knew Roland Sales, our backup running back, was good, and we had a very good offensive line. Our defense had some great players. Plus, Coach Holtz was pushing all the right buttons with us. We were confident."

Although the media portrayed the game as Goliath against a nearly weaponless David, Arkansas's players knew they had a solid game plan and a defense that could give OU's high-flying offense fits. Plus, in the finest era ever for collegiate long-distance kickers, Arkansas had the best in Little.

THE GAME
by Ron Calcagni

The Rose Bowl was running late, and we were being held in the dressing room as the Orange Bowl delayed its kickoff for network television. We were ready to play. We didn't want the delay. Coach Holtz did some magic tricks and then invited some of the players to talk. Roland Sales wasn't feeling very well, but he told us he was going to do his part to help. Once we got the word to come back out, Coach Holtz told us the last 22 out of the dressing room had to start the game.

As everyone else was running on the field, Coach Holtz held me back and said, "You and I are going last."

He told me to remember the plan: that I would carry the ball the first four plays. Then he said he and I were going to win this game. He would call the game from the sidelines, and I would call the plays on the field.

The game started perfectly for us. As always, Steve kicked off out of the end zone. On the third play from scrimmage the Sooners fumbled, and we recovered at OU's nine-yard line.

Sure enough, on the first play I ran off right tackle and picked up eight yards. Then Bruce Hay came in from the sidelines to bring us the play. He told me it was 34 Right. That is the running back. Load 34 is the quarterback. I asked him if he was sure, and he said yes. So, I handed the ball to Sales, and he scored the touchdown.

At first I didn't know what to think, but it didn't take long for me to realize what was going on. Coach Holtz already had me cranked up. Scoring a touchdown got Sales cranked up. After that Roland had a field day. We ran away from OU's strength, and Roland ran wild. He set an Orange Bowl record with 205 yards on 22 carries. He was named the game's Most Valuable Player.

I just continued to follow Coach Holtz's plan. We had a nice 58-yard drive, and I sneaked into the end zone from the one. OU had fumbled at our 42 before that drive started. Our defense gave them fits all night and caused several fumbles. With the field still wet, sometimes their backs just fell down.

It stayed 14-0 through halftime. We were feeling pretty good in the dressing room. We knew they had an explosive offense, but we were confident we could stop them. Coach Holtz wanted something positive to happen right away in the third quarter to keep the momentum in our favor.

Ron Calcagni

We didn't get a touchdown to start the third quarter, but Steve kicked a field goal, and we were ahead 17-0. He was a great kicker. It must have demoralized OU when he kept kicking off into the end zone. His kicking never allowed them to have any kind of good field position.

Later in the third quarter we drove 82 yards, and Roland scored from the four. It was 24-0, and we knew we had the game under control.

Then we gave them a glimmer of hope. We were marching again before I threw an interception. It didn't seem so bad, because it was picked off at their five-yard line, but they drove 95 yards for their only touchdown of the game.

They had one more drive in the fourth quarter, but we stopped them and Barnabas White scored near the end of the game to make it 31-6.

Looking back it's hard to believe I only threw 11 passes. I completed seven, and Roland caught four of them. It just shows what an incredible night he had. We ran for 315 yards against the No. 2 team in the nation, and Roland had over 200 by himself.

Our defense, of course, was great. They recovered three OU fumbles and made big plays all night.

Coach Holtz had developed a brilliant game plan. We knew their weaknesses. They never did slow us down.

POSTGAME

Because Arkansas had smashed the No. 2 team in the country and No. 1 Texas had lost to Notre Dame in the Cotton Bowl, Holtz lobbied for the national championship as soon as the Orange Bowl ended. It didn't happen. With its national power in the polls, Notre Dame leaped from fifth to first. Alabama, a winner over Ohio State in the Sugar Bowl, was second.

The Razorbacks finished the campaign ranked No. 3 in both polls. Holtz earned a national reputation as a disciplinarian, a master motivator, and a magician, even appearing with Johnny Carson on *The Tonight Show*.

Cowins, Forrest, and Bobo were reinstated in the spring of 1978. Cowins became the first Razorback ever to rush for more than 1,000 yards in three different seasons and is still Arkansas's career rushing leader.

Calcagni, Cowins, and Holtz were featured on the cover of *Sports Illustrated's* college football issue in September 1978 because the magazine picked the Hogs as number one. Midseason losses to Texas and Houston cost the Razorbacks a shot at No. 1, but they landed in the Fiesta Bowl where they tied UCLA.

WHAT HAPPENED TO RON CALCAGNI?

C alcagni married a Razorback cheerleader, Michelle. They have a daughter, Danielle, 18, and a son, Chase, 14. Ron played three years in the Canadian Football League before going into coaching. Larry Lacewell hired him on the staff at Arkansas State. He later served as an assistant coach at the University of Houston, Winnepeg of the CFL, Tulsa, Oklahoma State, and Oklahoma.

He now directs marketing for the Arkansas Twisters, an arena football team in Little Rock. Living in the state where he became a hero has kept the memory of the Orange Bowl alive for him.

"All these years later, everywhere I go that game has stayed with me," Calcagni says. "I've never been associated with a greater victory. It seems like it wasn't very long ago. I still see many of the guys who played on that team. It's a game I will never forget."

It's a game all of Arkansas will never forget.

CHAPTER 6

PRESTON CARPENTER

Born: January 1, 1934
Hometown: Muskogee, Oklahoma
Current Residence: Broken Arrow, Oklahoma
Occupation: Retired
Position: Blocking Back
Height: 6-2
Weight: 185
Years Lettered: 1953-1955
Accomplishments: Made *the* catch that allowed Arkansas to beat unbeaten Ole Miss at Little Rock in 1954; played linebacker and blocking back for the Razorbacks; made 50 career catches for 624 yards and seven touchdowns; was All-Southwest Conference in 1955.
Game: Arkansas vs. Ole Miss, October 23, 1954, at Little Rock, Arkansas

BACKGROUND

Preston Carpenter grew up everywhere.

"My father was in the Corps of Engineers. Until I was in the fourth grade we moved a lot. Then we moved to West Memphis and stayed there until I was a junior in high school."

His older brother, Lewis, was a terrific athlete, and they played a lot of sandlot football together. Carpenter loved baseball, too, and was playing American Legion ball by the time he was 13.

"Bill Terry was my coach," Carpenter recalls. "Baseball was my love. As I continued playing baseball, I eventually played against guys like Ken and Clete Boyer and Ralph Terry. I hit a home run to beat Ralph Terry one time.

"I played semipro baseball during the summers while I was in the NFL. In fact, I played in the Cleveland area until I was 35 years old. Jimmie Foxx was the coach of our semipro team."

During his junior year in high school his family moved to Muskogee, Oklahoma.

"We moved right in the middle of football season. Muskogee had a great team. I went out for the team on a Monday and started that Friday night."

He only went to school at Muskogee for a year and a half but made the all-century Oklahoma high school all-star team.

His brother, meanwhile, already was at Arkansas. Carpenter, though, was leaning toward playing football at Oklahoma.

"Pete Smith owned a restaurant in Muskogee and was a big OU fan," Carpenter says. "He would fly me with him to the OU games. I was going there, but two weeks before I was leaving Otis Douglas, the Arkansas coach at the time, visited me. He convinced me to change my mind."

Carpenter was a freshman when Lewis was a senior. They never had the opportunity to play on the same team together at Arkansas. Early in his college life Carpenter decided to get married.

"I was getting married, and Otis Douglas got fired. Bowden Wyatt was hired as head coach, and he didn't permit married players. I called Bud Wilkenson at OU, and he was willing to fly a plane over and pick me up.

"I told John Barnhill, our athletic director, that Coach Wyatt didn't want me. Coach Barnhill took me with him to see Coach Wyatt. He told Bowden that I would be at Arkansas longer than he would. Bowden Wyatt never said another word to me, but I stayed and played. Jenne and I got married, and we've been married 52 years."

Carpenter admits he didn't care much for the classroom.

"I went to Arkansas to play football, not go to school," he confesses. "I didn't like school. I flunked Western Civ my freshman year. On our last day of class that year I told my teacher, Mr. Ryan, I couldn't take the test. I got in my car and drove to New Mexico to play baseball for the summer.

"I only passed eight of 16 hours the second semester of my first year. I had to take a correspondence course to be eligible as a sophomore. Back then you only had to pass nine hours to be able to play.

"We had changed coaches, but football doesn't change. You have to go out and win no matter who the coach is. That's the approach I took in high school, college, and the pros. It was all football to me."

In 1953 the Razorbacks won only three games in Wyatt's first year. Carpenter played linebacker and was a blocking back on offense. He liked defense best.

"I caught a lot of swing passes coming out of the backfield, but I mostly blocked on offense. I loved playing linebacker. I wanted to play linebacker in the pros, but they never let me. I was All-Southwest Conference as a linebacker at Arkansas.

"I was a better defensive player than offense. I had great instinct. I would blitz before anyone knew what a blitz was. The coaches would ask me what I was doing. I just knew where the play was going and went after the ball.

"Even though Coach Wyatt didn't like me, I played every down in 1953. I don't remember many of the details of that season, because I played so many games in college and the pros. I just remember the coaches told me what to do, and I did it.

"There are all those stories about how tough Wyatt was, but he never hit me. His practices were tough, though. I remember being at a banquet one time with eight of the Junction Boys from Bear Bryant's days at Texas A&M. I was struck by how small most of them were. I told them Junction wasn't anything compared to Bowden Wyatt's training camp. They all looked at me funny."

THE SEASON

In 1954 few of the football experts thought much of Arkansas's chances in the Southwest Conference. Wyatt had reduced the Razorbacks to a smaller squad with his difficult training camps, and the Hogs had not won more than five games in a season since 1947. The 1954 Razorbacks would become known as "the 25 Little Pigs."

"Maybe no one else thought we would be any good, but I never thought about it. It was one of those years. We just played. I remember three games real well—Baylor, Texas, and Ole Miss. Other than that I don't remember all the details. A lot of guys on that team can tell you practically every play of the year.

"I do know it was the first time Arkansas ever won every road game we played in Texas. We beat TCU, Texas, and Texas A&M. Houston wasn't in the Southwest Conference, but we beat them on the road, too."

Arkansas opened the season with wins over Tulsa and TCU before visiting Baylor. The Razorbacks trailed 20-18 in the fourth quarter after missing all three extra points.

"We didn't have anyone who could kick very well," Carpenter says. "I missed an extra point, and two other guys missed them, too. We got close to their goal line in the fourth quarter, and Bowden asked me if I could kick a 15-yard field goal. I said sure. I made it, and we won 21-20. It was the only field goal of my career."

The following week the Hogs earned their first win at Texas since 1937.

"Texas was big. They were much bigger than we were. I scored our first touchdown by intercepting a pass and running about 21 yards for the score. After that Henry Moore beat them. The rest of us just played. Henry had a long touchdown run and just pounded them."

The Hogs won 20-7 to improve their record to 4-0.

THE SCENE

In the 1950s and 1960s, Ole Miss was a national power. The Rebels were unbeaten and almost impossible to score against when they came to Little Rock for the 1954 game. But Carpenter had no fear.

"I treated Ole Miss like any other game. I treated football like it was a job. Practicing was like going to work. Every game was the same to me. I was always ready. I just wanted to play.

"I wanted to play so bad I played with a separated shoulder for two years in college. Our trainer, Bill Farrell, would tape my arm to my side so my shoulder would stay in place. I didn't want to miss a play. I bent a finger back real bad one time. Bill taped it in place and told me I was ready to go."

Although Carpenter didn't think of Ole Miss as more important than other opponents, Razorback fans did. They waited all week for the game and jammed War Memorial Stadium in Little Rock to capacity.

"Kids today listen to all the hype," Carpenter says. "I never paid any attention to all that stuff in the press. All I remember is we stayed in Hot Springs, like we always did before a Little Rock game, bussed to the game, and played. Later in my pro career I went over the opponent's personnel, but I didn't know many of the players on Ole Miss's team. I just knew they were good."

THE GAME
by Preston Carpenter

I still have the game on two reels of reel-to-reel film. I've watched it several times. The first three quarters were all defense. We just kept stopping each other and trading punts. Ole Miss had a great defense, and we had a very good defense, too.

Back then you didn't have that many plays in a game. It seemed like there were only 38 to 40 plays in a game. It was probably more than that. I just remember we went back and forth with no one scoring. I caught a couple of swing passes out of the backfield, but for the most part I just blocked.

In the fourth quarter, about five plays before we finally scored, I remember really hitting an Ole Miss ball carrier. It was a hard tackle. That was unusual back then. There weren't many hard, hard hits. I remember playing a high school game against Oklahoma City Capital Hill one time. They were supposed to be real good. I don't think there was a tackle made in the entire game. Backs would just run into the pile at the line of scrimmage, and eventually they'd blow the ball dead.

Anyway, when we got the ball back, Wyatt put the second group in the game. We had a first group and a second group. Buddy Bob Benson, Ronnie Underwood, and Joe Bill Wilson were in there. I was in there with them.

Looking back, everyone talks about the Powder River Play that won the game. To tell you the truth, I had never heard of a Powder River Play. I hadn't heard of it referred to in that way. I guess I should have known, since I'm the one who caught it.

As a blocking back, the only passes I usually caught were swing passes out of the backfield. On this particular play I eased off tackle and went downfield. Buddy Bob Benson ran to the weak side, then turned, and threw the ball.

I had 4.7 speed in the 40, but everyone always told me I was too slow. I was the second slowest back at Arkansas. We had some fast backs. But Billy Kinard was covering me, and I was behind him. I caught the ball and ran into the end zone. Billy was a rookie with the Browns the same year I was. I reminded him of being behind him for the touchdown.

After the game I couldn't even remember what end zone it was. Everyone reminds me it was the north end zone. I've already mentioned we didn't have anyone who could kick very well. We missed the extra point and won 6-0.

All the people came out of the stands after the game and wanted to put me on their shoulders. Everyone was celebrating, but it was just another game to me.

Preston Carpenter

POSTGAME

Arkansas followed its monumental upset of Ole Miss with victories over Texas A&M and Rice but lost two of its last three regular-season games before meeting Georgia Tech in the Cotton Bowl.

Frank Broyles was the Georgia Tech offensive coordinator for head coach Bobby Dodd, and the Yellow Jackets beat the Hogs 14-6 at Dallas.

"I missed the second half of the game with an injury," Carpenter explains. "I was told later that Tech wanted me out of the game to help them have a better chance of winning."

Wyatt left after the charmed season of 1954, and Jack Mitchell was the new coach. Carpenter was a co-captain on a team that finished 5-4-1.

"I missed the first game of the 1955 season," Carpenter recalls. "They tackled me on my left knee in the preseason. I only missed one game and was lucky that I never had a knee problem after that. We had a pretty good year and would have gone to the Sugar Bowl if we had beaten LSU in the last game of the season. They upset us at Little Rock, and our season was over."

Despite his disinterest in school, he earned his degree by taking 21 hours per semester at the end.

"I wasn't a good student, but I did finish. Somehow I passed."

WHAT HAPPENED TO PRESTON CARPENTER?

Carpenter's football career was far from over. A first-round draft choice of the Cleveland Browns, he spent 12 years in the National Football League. He played four years for the Browns, four with the Pittsburgh Steelers, and three with the Washington Redskins and finished with the Dolphins and Vikings. During his first season in Cleveland, the Browns had 75 rookies in their camp. He was one of five who made the team.

"I never missed an offensive play in 12 years," Carpenter says. "In fact, I never missed a practice. I was fortunate to stay healthy. I became a tight end in 1957, the first year the NFL started using tight ends."

He also returned punts and kickoffs and led the NFL in punt returns in 1960. He made the All-Pro team in 1962, the only year the team was picked by NFL players rather than the media.

The Browns reached the 1957 NFL Championship Game with Carpenter at tight end. A year later he caught nine third-down passes in one game against the Baltimore Colts. Once, when he was with Pittsburgh, he caught three touchdown passes in the game's first three minutes.

"The kept fumbling after we would score," he recalls. "Later in the game I dropped a pass. To my knowledge it was the only pass I dropped in my entire pro career."

He earned 5,400 receiving yards before he retired. His motto throughout his career was, "I'm gonna hit thee before you hit me."

When his football career ended, he went into the trucking business. His wife, Jenne, had a bout with cancer "but is through it now." He has three sons, Scott, Bruce, and Todd, who led the state in rushing as a running back at Conway. Todd also played football at Air Force for coach Ken Hatfield.

Carpenter plays golf almost daily, sees his brother Lewis as often as possible, and returns frequently for Razorback events. He was asked to coach football in Austria in 2004 and spent 10 days there before returning to help take care of Jenne, who was battling cancer at the time.

CHAPTER 7

RONNIE CAVENESS

Born: March 6, 1943
Hometown: Houston, Texas
Current Residence: Little Rock
Occupation: Sales for Dealers Truck Equipment
Position: Linebacker
Height: 6-0
Weight: 210
Years Lettered: 1962-1964
Accomplishments: Was a consensus All-American in 1964; was twice named All-Southwest Conference; still holds Arkansas's career record for tackles in a game with 29 against Texas in 1963; made 25 tackles versus Texas in 1964, the second highest total ever by a Hog; ranks fifth on the UA career tackle list with 357; made 155 tackles in 1964 and 154 in 1963, the third and fourth best single-season efforts ever by a Razorback.
The Game: Arkansas vs. Tulsa, September 26, 1964, at Fayetteville, Arkansas

BACKGROUND

Until he enrolled at Arkansas, Ronnie Caveness was always bigger than other young men in his age group. In fact, when he was in the seventh grade, he played on his ninth-grade team.

"The coaches thought it would be good for me to play against kids my own size and maybe a little bigger," Caveness recalls. "I thought it would be fun. Instead it was pretty rough."

It wasn't rough enough to discourage him, though, and by the time he reached high school he found a mentor in Buzzy Allert, his position coach.

"Coach Allert took me under his wing," Caveness says. "He pushed me and encouraged me. I played linebacker and offensive guard. Jerry Lamb was on my team. He was a year ahead of me. He redshirted at Arkansas, and I didn't. That's why we were in the same senior class as Razorbacks.

"I always needed someone to lead me. Jerry and Coach Allert set the pace for me. It was hard to keep up. Plus, the Houston area has so many good teams; we were playing tough games every week.

"Before my senior year, our school moved to District 12 4-A. It was like a little Southwest Conference. It was the best district in Texas at the time. Coach Allert was elevated to head coach before that season.

"He was tough. We started the year with 50 players and were down to 19 by our season opener. We didn't win a game. It didn't change his approach, though. We were called the 'Tough 20,' because we had one teammate who had a broken arm and couldn't play. We would play for pride no matter what the score. We still have a reunion of that group every year."

Fortunately for Caveness, Lamb told Arkansas's coaches about him, and the Razorbacks were the only team to recruit him for the longest time. He signed with the Hogs and was ready to head for Fayetteville.

At that time, though, each conference had its own letter of intent, and it was binding only in that league. Alabama had been recruiting an opponent of Caveness's high school but liked what it saw of Caveness on film.

"Alabama invited me to visit," Caveness says. "I did, liked it, and signed with them. Coach [Frank] Broyles resolved it. He came to visit and had a copy of Dave Campbell's *Texas Football* magazine. He said I would be in the magazine and would be an All-American. I told that to my dad, and he said I should stick with my original commitment to Arkansas. I couldn't call coach [Bear] Bryant. I never told them I wasn't coming. I just went to Arkansas."

Caveness enrolled in the fall of 1961. He was quickly introduced to legendary Razorback assistant coach Wilson Matthews.

"During the recruiting process I was made to feel important," Caveness explains. "Everyone wanted me. I thought I was pretty big stuff. At that time the freshmen practiced on the lower field. Coach Matthews came down and called me over to a tackling drill.

"He brought a big physical running back to the drill. I'll never forget it. He didn't have any teeth. He had us both back up and run right at each other. I hit the guy, and my lights went out. I remember looking up, and there was Coach Matthews. He was smiling and said, 'Recruiting is over.'"

As a sophomore in 1962, Caveness started at center and linebacker. The Hogs finished the regular season 9-1 before losing to Ole Miss in the Sugar Bowl.

"My sophomore year was a lot of fun. Billy Moore was our quarterback. He was an All-American that season. We had Texas beat at Austin but fumbled into their end zone, and they pulled it out with a long scoring drive at the end of the game. Playing in the Sugar Bowl was very exciting. Ole Miss was really good and beat us, but we finished that year thinking we would be very good in 1963."

But his junior season didn't turn out quite like he expected.

"It was the weirdest season I ever played," Caveness recalls. "We had a lot of seniors, and our junior class was very good. We were picked to walk through the conference. During two-a-days, though, we had several guys get hurt, and for some reason we never jelled. We rotated three quarterbacks, Freddie Marshall, Bill Gray, and Jon Brittenum.

"The defense spent too much time on the field. Eventually we wore down. We worked just as hard but couldn't find a way to win."

The Hogs finished 5-5 with every loss by seven points or less. A victory over Texas Tech in the regular-season finale at least gave the Razorbacks a little momentum heading into 1964.

THE SEASON

Arkansas's seniors prepared diligently to make sure there was no repeat of the 1963 season. Still, there were no guarantees as the Razorbacks prepared for what would be their greatest season.

"As a defense we hadn't played together much," Caveness says. "I started the previous year, but most of the others had not. Normally Coach Broyles didn't have the seniors participate in spring practice. In the spring of 1964 our seniors did practice. Coach wanted us to begin working together. That was a big factor. We got to know each other better.

"We had 10 or 12 seniors, and we came together as a group. There was a feeling of urgency. Going 5-5 just wasn't going to cut it. We knew we had to go to work. Even before spring practice Coach Matthews put us through fourth-quarter conditioning. Every day we built a working attitude.

"One of the most important things that happened early was settling on one quarterback. Freddie Marshall would be the quarterback. Bill Gray would play defense, and they redshirted Jon Brittenum. They weren't going to rotate like they did in 1963. That really helped."

Although expectations were high among the Razorbacks, little was expected by those who made preseason predictions. Watching the SWC favorites in 1963 stagger to a 5-5 finish convinced most of the experts to pick defending national champion Texas to win with several others ahead of the Hogs.

"No one picked us this time," Caveness says. "We were picked down in the league. Personally I was glad to see that. We were under no pressure at all."

The Hogs opened with Oklahoma State. Walt Garrison, the Cowboys' outstanding fullback who later starred for the Dallas Cowboys, gave the Razorbacks fits, but somehow Arkansas managed to earn a 14-10 victory.

"We learned a lot about ourselves against Oklahoma State," Caveness says. "We played together as a unit. The game was close, but we got through it. We were getting to know each other, and we moved forward."

THE SCENE

A rkansas and Tulsa first met in 1922 and they became regular opponents in the early 1930s. Except for a brief period in the 1940s when the Hurricane became a national power, the Razorbacks generally won with many of the games going down to the wire.

"We beat Tulsa pretty handily my first two years, but this time they had a quarterback named Jerry Rhome and a receiver named Howard Twilley. Those guys were outstanding. We could tell that by looking at their statistics. We respected Tulsa but knew they really didn't play anybody.

"All week we worked on defending Rhome and their great passing game. We knew if we let them get started, we would be playing on our heels."

Arkansas was ranked 11th in the country when Tulsa visited Razorback Stadium. A slipup against the Hurricane likely would have knocked the Hogs out of the top 20.

THE GAME
by Ronnie Caveness

A ll week we worked on Tulsa's passing game, but in the first quarter they really mixed it up. They ran when we thought they would pass, and about the time we thought they would run, they'd pass. They kept us off balance. It was great play-calling.

When the first quarter ended, we were down 14-0. We were all looking at each other. It was spooky. The crowd was shocked. As usual we had a stadium full of people, but they were quiet.

Ronnie Caveness

Coach Matthews always told us to do something or hit someone in order to create something positive for our team. In the second quarter I decided to do something.

Tulsa had wide splits between their offensive linemen. That was unusual back then. It was also unusual to blitz. Hardly anyone knew what that was. I thought I would run through one of their splits and make something happen in the backfield.

"I blew past the offensive guard as Rhome was pitching to his halfback. I started toward the back, but he stopped and raised his arm. I slowed up and was about 10 yards from him. The ball slipped out of his hands, and he threw a duck. I reached up and grabbed it. If we ever needed a touchdown, it was then. I ran 12 yards into the end zone.

We ran a 5-4 defense, and, as I said earlier, we never blitzed. They didn't expect a linebacker to come into their backfield. The halfback panicked. I was just trying to make something happen, because up to that point whatever we were doing wasn't working.

Years later I ran into Rhome in an airport. We visited about the game, and he told me the guy who threw that pass never played another down the rest of the year.

Now we were behind 14-7. On the first play of the next series, I acted like I was going to hit another gap. I was showing them another different look. Rhome pulled out from center too fast, and the next thing I knew the ball was right at my feet. I fell on it, and we ended up kicking a field goal. That made it 14-10 at the half. The crowd got back in the game, and we were feeling a lot better.

I didn't grow up in Arkansas, but I had learned how important Razorback fans are to their team. Arkansas has great tradition, and its fans love to win. There has always been a strong connection between the fans and the team. They make all the difference in a game. Really and truly, that's for whom the players are playing. When you win, everyone feels great.

After my career at Arkansas was over, I had the opportunity to play in some all-star games and in the pros. Other players would tell me how great our fans were. Larry Cramer, who played at Nebraska and against us in the 1965 Cotton Bowl, was particularly complimentary of our fans. I was thinking their fans were very good, too.

Anyway, once the fans were back in the game, we knew we had a good chance to win. It was quiet in the dressing room, but we could feel the momentum. Coach [Doug] Dickey was our offensive coordinator. He said the best defense against a team like Tulsa was to keep our defense off the field.

In the second half we opened it up. Bill Gray came in at quarterback and hit a big pass to Jerry Lamb to start the third quarter. That was the game that showed us we could pass the ball. Our offense kept Rhome on the sidelines for much of the second half.

When Tulsa had the ball, they were doing the same things they did in the first half, but those passes weren't being completed. We went to another level. I can't explain it. I just remember we could feel the crowd, and we played football. We were quicker to the ball.

There are so many intangibles involved in football. There is so much mental work to the game. It's not all Xs and Os. Ronnie Mac Smith was one of our other linebackers. Early in the game we were both acting like we weren't worried, but we wondered what was going on.

By the end of the game, we had a better feeling. Tulsa didn't score again until late, and by then we had 31 points. We had found out more about our team as we were preparing for the Southwest Conference season. Beating Tulsa was a real confidence builder for us.

POSTGAME

Tulsa was the only team to score more than two touchdowns on Arkansas all year. In fact, after a 14-13 victory at Texas, the Razorbacks didn't allow another point in their last five regular-season games.

"Our defense was very confident, especially after beating Texas," Caveness admits. "Our group had never beaten Texas. After that win, we were a different team. Our defense had a lot of pride. We not only wanted to shut out our opponents, we wanted to hold them to three downs and get their offense off the field.

"We had one big challenge in our last regular-season game. Texas Tech had Donny Anderson, a great running back. They had just one loss, and if they had beaten us, they would have tied us for the league championship and gone to the Cotton Bowl. They were fired up. Just like Tulsa, they went up and down the field against us, but Bobby Roper blocked three field goals, and we won the game 17-0."

Arkansas was 10-0 and ranked second nationally before its Cotton Bowl date with Nebraska. The Huskers were 9-1 after losing their regular-season finale to Oklahoma.

"We never thought much about winning a national championship," Caveness confesses. "We were just getting ready for Nebraska. They were huge. Our offensive tackles weighed 220 pounds. Jimmy Johnson, our nose guard, played at 200. Quickness was our asset. Their tackles were 270, and they had a running back, Harry Wilson, who was 220. They were tough.

"Football players can get religion before a game. Both teams came down the tunnel at the Cotton Bowl at the same time. They were popping out of their jerseys, and we didn't fill ours. I said, 'Lord, we need help.'"

Arkansas defeated Nebraska 10-7, and No. 1 Alabama lost in the Orange Bowl to Texas. The Razorbacks were awarded the post-bowl versions of the national championship.

"We took a lot of pride in being the only undefeated team in college football that year," Caveness says. "The trophies are still on display, and the memories have lasted a lifetime. Our team had a special bond and still does to this day."

WHAT HAPPENED TO RONNIE CAVENESS?

Caveness was drafted by Kansas City in the old American Football League and by the Los Angeles Rams of the National Football League. He signed with the Chiefs, spent a year there, and then went to Miami. The Houston Oilers traded for him, and he finished his career with the Patriots.

"A knee injury ended my career," he says. "I had been spending the offseasons in Little Rock working on my degree at Arkansas–Little Rock. When I finished my education, I went to work for my father-in-law at Coleman Dairy and was there 10 years."

Now Caveness sells for Dealers Truck Equipment in Little Rock. He is married to Teresa. His son, Ronnie Jr., lives in Fayetteville, and his daughter is a dance teacher in Little Rock. He still remembers his days at Arkansas fondly.

"My time at Arkansas was the best experience of my life. I thank Coach Broyles for coming and getting me. It was really something that my senior year in high school we were 0-10, and my senior year at Arkansas we were 11-0. At our 40-year reunion Coach Broyles used the word *love* in describing what our group had. Old players don't talk about that much, but he was right. We had it then, and we've still got it today."

CHAPTER 8

BOBBY CROCKETT

Born: April 3, 1943
Hometown: Dermott
Current Residence: Harriett
Occupation: Convenience Store and Canoe Rental Owner
Position: Wide Receiver
Height: 6-2
Weight: 195
Years Lettered: 1963-1965
Accomplishments: Was All-American, 1965, All-Southwest Conference, 1965; caught 30 passes for 487 yards and three touchdowns in 1965 after making seven catches for 121 yards and a touchdown in 1964; was a starter during Arkansas's school-record 22-game winning streak and helped the Hogs go 10-0 during the 1964 and 1965 regular seasons.
The Game: Arkansas vs. Texas, October 16, 1965, at Fayetteville, Arkansas

BACKGROUND

At the time Bobby Crockett was growing up in southeast Arkansas, every young man in every corner of the state wanted to be a Razorback. Frank Broyles had built a powerful program after his arrival in December 1957, and a statewide radio network brought the play-by-play of every Hog game into homes and cars everywhere in Arkansas.

"I was one of those who wanted to be a Razorback," Crockett recalls. "There weren't many of us from southeast Arkansas going to Fayetteville. Football in our area was just all right. Senator Matt Gibson from our area talked to the coaching staff about giving me a scholarship. I worked hard for that scholarship but probably wouldn't have received it without Senator Gibson."

Before he could become one of the greatest receivers in Razorback history, Crockett had to become eligible. That was a challenge.

"My freshman year I passed seven out of 30 hours," Crockett says. "I had to redshirt in my second year because I wasn't eligible to play. As a freshman I had been on the black squad, which was dead last, and the blue squad, which was next to last. We had a lot more players then than they do now, and it took a lot of endurance to work your way into playing time.

"During my second year I moved up to the orange squad. That was the suicide squad. We practiced against the starting defense every day. We ran the opponent's plays. If we did well, we had to run the play again. We would run the play over and over until the defense stopped us.

"The thing I remember most about that redshirt year was the practice before spring break. Ronnie Caveness was from Houston. I was going home with him, and then we were going to Galveston. We were already packed before practice.

"I was a tailback then, and that was the day they decided to see if I would stay with the football team. I ran every play for both sides. They were seeing if I was tough enough. It was terrible. But I came back. I never thought of leaving."

Later he was moved to wide receiver. He played during the disappointing 1963 season when the Hogs were picked to compete for the Southwest Conference championship but instead finished 5-5.

"We came back determined to have a better year in 1964," Crockett says. "We never could have imagined winning the national championship. No one picked us to do very well. We struggled through some of our early games, but our game at Texas became the key to the season."

Texas was the defending national champion and ranked No. 1 when Arkansas arrived in Austin in October 1964. Ken Hatfield's long punt return gave the Hogs a lead by the Longhorns tied the game at 7-7 when Crockett made one of the biggest plays of his career.

"Texas was playing us real tight on the out pattern," he recalls. "We called the play, and the defensive back came up quick, allowing me to break free. Fortunately Fred Marshall saw me and hit me with the pass."

The result was a 34-yard touchdown that made the score 14-7. Texas scored in the last minute but was stopped on a two-point try. The Razorbacks didn't allow another score in their last five regular-season games and beat Nebraska in the Cotton Bowl to emerge as the only unbeaten team in college football.

THE SEASON

The next year Arkansas opened the season on a 12-game winning streak. Expectations were high. The Hogs suffered heavy graduation losses but still had plenty of talent coming back. The offense, in particular, was extremely optimistic.

"Our defense in 1964 was unbelievable," Crockett says. "They just stopped everybody. We lost some of our best defensive players, but the success we had in 1964 led us to believe we would win every game in 1965. We had a winning tradition going. We were very confident."

Crockett's wide receiver coach was a young Barry Switzer, who had played center at Arkansas just six years earlier.

"Barry was a motivator," Crockett recalls. "He coached tight ends and wide receivers. I was the oldest receiver on that team. He said to me, 'You know what to do, don't you?' I did because I had played so much, so he didn't coach me much. But again, he was a heckuva motivator."

Featuring Bobby Burnett and lightning-fast Harry Jones in the backfield with quarterback Jon Brittenum, Arkansas's offense started quickly, averaging 29 points per game in victories over Oklahoma State, Tulsa, Texas Christian University, and Baylor.

The defense was still formidable as well. The Hogs shut out TCU and surrendered just a touchdown against Baylor.

THE SCENE

By 1965 the Arkansas–Texas rivalry was regarded as one of the best in the country. It was right up there with USC–Notre Dame and Oklahoma–Texas. It was much bigger than Alabama–Auburn was at that time. NBC had college football at the time and televised the 1965 game from Fayetteville to the entire nation. (During the 1960s there was just one college telecast per week.)

"Playing Texas was always big, but the rivalry intensified in the mid-1960s, because both teams were always ranked high," Crockett says. "Our players loved playing Texas. Both teams played with class. It was always a clean game.

"After we beat them in 1964, we were excited about playing Texas in Fayetteville. We were totally focused all week. There was so much hype that week. We were all excited. I remember being outside our dressing room before the game with Jon Brittenum. We loved seeing so many fans with such enthusiasm. We always had great crowds, but when we played Texas at home, it was extra special.

"I've been to a lot of Razorback games since that day in 1965, including the 2004 Texas game, which set a school record for attendance. I don't think I've ever been in a more electrifying atmosphere than Razorback Stadium for the 1965 Texas game. In my mind the 42,000 fans who were there were even more energized than the 2004 crowd. Don't get me wrong. That 2004 crowd was electric. I just remember the 1965 crowd being the greatest ever. The atmosphere was explosive."

The Hogs had defeated Texas the previous year, and the Longhorns hadn't lost again in 1964 and helped the Razorbacks win the national title by defeating Alabama in the Orange Bowl. Coming into the 1965 matchup, they again were ranked No. 1. Arkansas was highly regarded as well, holding down the No. 3 spot in the national polls.

THE GAME
by Bobby Crockett

It couldn't have started better for us. On our second possession Jon Brittenum threw me a little swing pass, and it turned into a 58-yard touchdown. We were excited until we saw the penalty flag on the ground. The play was called back, and we had to punt.

It's funny, but I had almost forgotten that play. I had never seen it until we saw a replay of the entire game while filming a Razorback Classic television show. The only plays I had seen much of since the game itself were the ones on the last drive.

We would have loved the early touchdown but got one anyway when Texas fumbled the punt and it bounced into the end zone where Martine Bercher jumped on it. Martine was a great defensive back and made All-American in 1966. In fact, he made a big interception to help Arkansas beat Texas the next year in Austin. He played on teams that never lost to Texas. There aren't many of us who can say that.

Texas had a great offense, and they came right back down the field. They were just about to score when they fumbled a handoff into the air. Tommy Trantham was right there. At that time a fumble couldn't be advanced once it touched the ground. Tommy caught the loose ball and headed in the other direction. I don't think a Texas player ever got anywhere near him. He ended up running 77 yards, and we were ahead by two touchdowns.

Early in the second quarter we finally had a good drive against them. Jon hit me in the end zone for the touchdown. Again, it was just a vague memory until taping that television show. That gave us a 20-0 lead, but that's not the touchdown you ever see when they are showing the old highlights.

Bobby Crockett

We missed the extra point, but it hardly looked like it would matter. In the 1960s it was very hard to overcome a 20-point lead. Teams didn't pass as much as they do today.

The defense scored so easily, we might have become overconfident. Once we had a 20-point lead, what little offense we had shown up to that point we shut down. We were playing just to hold the lead.

Before the half Texas came back on us. They kicked a field goal, then scored a touchdown and made the two-point conversion. We had a hard time stopping them after that. One thing about Texas, they never gave up. They kicked a field goal, then scored a touchdown, and kicked another field goal in the fourth quarter, and we were behind. That 20-0 lead seemed like a long time ago. When we got the ball at our 20 with little more than four minutes left, we knew it would be our last chance to win.

Coach Broyles asked me if I could get open. I thought I could before, and I thought I could at that point. He told me they would throw it to me all the way down the field.

Not every play of that drive came to me, but it sure seemed like it. We kept running the same pattern. The catches were pretty ordinary. It was throwing and catching, just like in practice. The only difference was it was happening in the biggest game of the year.

We got to their 11, and Jon threw me a pass near the sideline. I was able to catch it and get a foot down before going out at the one. I didn't think there was anything special about that catch, but people talk about it even today.

Jon could really throw the football. I played in the Senior Bowl, the All-American Bowl, and with the Buffalo Bills in the NFL, and I think Jon Brittenum was the best quarterback I ever saw. He could be running right and throw back to the left on a line. He had a heckuva arm. He wasn't a great drop-back passer, but he could really throw the sprint-out passes.

Anyway, Jon ran a quarterback sneak for the touchdown. There was about a minute and a half left. The crowd was very loud, and Texas wasn't great at scoring in a hurry. We intercepted a pass before Texas could really get started and then ran the clock out.

POSTGAME

Arkansas won out to finish the regular season 10-0. The Hogs were ranked second nationally behind Michigan State. The Razorbacks could have made it two national championships in a row with a victory over LSU in the Cotton Bowl, but Brittenum separated his shoulder in the first half, and the Tigers ended Arkansas's 22-game winning streak with a 14-7 upset. It was especially difficult to take, because the top-ranked Spartans lost to UCLA in the Rose Bowl.

WHAT HAPPENED TO
BOBBY CROCKETT?

Crockett was drafted by Buffalo and spent four years with the Bills. He was the American Football League's rookie of the year in 1966 when he caught 31 passes for 533 yards and three touchdowns. He averaged 17.2 yards per catch.

Injuries shortened his pro career. He finished during the 1969 season with career totals of 41 receptions for 659 yards.

He had completed his undergraduate degree at Arkansas Tech and started law school at the UA while with the Bills. In 1972 he graduated from law school and began practicing in Clinton. He was there for 17 years before he found a convenience store and canoe rental for sale near the Buffalo River. He made the purchase and has been there since.

"It is a great way to spend my years," Crockett says. "It's only about two and a half hours from Fayetteville, and I get back for games. It's changed a lot, of course. It's great when some of us are able to get together and rehash old times."

Crockett has three adult sons, Bobby Paul, who is a junior high football coach in Fayetteville; Hayden; and Creed.

CHAPTER 9

CHUCK DICUS

Born: October 2, 1948
Hometown: Garland, Texas
Current Residence: Fayetteville
Occupation: President, Razorback Foundation
Position: Wide Receiver
Height: 6-1
Weight: 185
Years Lettered: 1968-1970
Accomplishments: Was an All-American two times and All-Southwest Conference three times; made 118 career catches for 1,854 yards and 16 touchdowns, all school records when he finished at Arkansas; was MVP of the 1969 Sugar Bowl with 12 catches for 169 yards; still ranks in the top 10 in every category of Arkansas's career receiving list.
The Game: Arkansas vs. Georgia, January 1, 1969, Sugar Bowl at New Orleans, Louisiana

BACKGROUND

His father was a football coach for only three years, but Chuck Dicus was greatly influenced by his dad's time at Texarkana (Texas) High School. Two of Texarkana's best, James Monroe and George McKinney, crossed the border and played football at the University of Arkansas.

Dicus's dad became a Razorback fan as he followed the careers of his former players. Chuck was four, five, and six years old during his father's coaching days and fell under the spell of the Hogs at an early age.

When Dicus was in the third grade, his family settled in Garland, a suburb of Dallas. With McKinney at quarterback, Arkansas won the Southwest Conference title in 1960, and the Razorbacks were the host team in the Cotton Bowl. Dicus and his dad visited McKinney at the team hotel and had tickets for the game against Duke.

Surrounded by Razorback followers at the bowl game, his first college football experience, Dicus was hooked for life. He was devoted to following Arkansas football.

During his freshman and sophomore years of high school, Garland won state football championships. Dicus was a quarterback but didn't play on the varsity those two years. Then the school split and Dicus's junior team was 3-6-1 with him at the helm. It was a little better his senior season when his squad was 6-3-1.

Dicus was a five-foot-11, 160-pound quarterback who threw "only when I was about to be sacked" and played in the same district as future Razorback star and teammate Bill Montgomery and Eddie Phillips, a future Texas Longhorn great.

"I didn't get many honors," Dicus recalls. "I think I was honorable mention All-Dallas. I didn't get much recruiting attention, either. People weren't looking for a quarterback my size."

His first recruiting trip was to McMurray College in Abilene, Texas.

"I wanted to go to Arkansas but didn't get any attention from them," he explains.

"I visited McMurray with a high school teammate. When we arrived at Abilene, I thought surely I wouldn't have to go to college there. They offered us both scholarships, and my teammate accepted and had a good career there."

During his senior season Dicus had two long scoring runs to help his team beat Mesquite.

"I told a sportswriter that I was an Arkansas fan, and it was in the paper the next day," Dicus recalls. "A man named Wiley Thornton, a member of the Dallas Razorback Club who didn't know me, saw the article and sent it to Johnny Majors, who was an assistant coach at Arkansas. Coach Majors called me but not much happened after that."

After his senior campaign Dicus decided he needed to get bigger, so he went on a weight-lifting program and gained 10 pounds. Oklahoma State got interested and invited him to visit Stillwater.

"I flew to Stillwater on a single-engine plane," Dicus says. "There was another plane coming, so we waited at the airport. Mike Kelson and Steve Vestal were on the plane coming from Houston. Kelson was the biggest human I'd ever seen at that point in my life. Ironically, all three of us ended up at Arkansas, and there we were visiting Oklahoma State on the same weekend.

"They showed us around and told us we would go to a wrestling match that night. I couldn't believe it. The only thing I knew about wrestling was the Friday night kind of pro wrestling. It was a big deal there.

"They wanted me to commit on the visit and told me they wanted to develop me as a quarterback. I didn't think my arm was strong enough and thought my chances were better as a wide receiver or defensive back.

"I didn't commit, and when I got home, I had a message to call Coach Majors. He invited me to visit Fayetteville the next weekend. When coach [Frank] Broyles saw me and greeted me by name on my visit, I would have signed on the spot.

"I think the extra 10 pounds I had added helped convince them, but I've always wondered if they recruited me just to room with Montgomery. He was the only person at the University of Arkansas who I knew."

As a freshman in the fall of 1967, Dicus was scared.

"No one had prepared me for college life," he says. "I had high anxiety. A month before we were to report, I had a motorcycle accident, and I couldn't get in shape. I was afraid they would send me home.

"They were patient, and I got well. I played defensive back until midway through my freshman season. Our freshman team played five games, and I didn't start any of them. I moved to receiver and was behind David Carter. He was from Fort Smith, and he was the big signee of our class. I caught a few passes at Tulsa and gained some confidence from that.

"After the season we had some big coaching changes. Coach Broyles brought in Don Breaux as offensive coordinator and Richard Williamson to coach receivers. We went to a pro passing attack with split backs and wideouts.

"In the spring we had Max Peacock, David Cox, and a bunch of us younger guys. Richard Williamson molded me into a wide receiver. He came from Alabama where he had worked with Ray Perkins and Dennis Holman, both All-Americans. He was the most hard-nosed, demanding coach I had ever been around. I responded positively and earned a starting spot that spring."

THE SEASON

After winning 22 games in a row, two Southwest Conference championships, and a national title, Arkansas fell to 4-5-1 in 1967. When the 1968 season opened, no one knew how good the Razorbacks might be. For the first time since he came to Fayetteville, Broyles started a sophomore quarterback (Montgomery) in the season opener. Dicus and tailback Bill Burnett also were sophomores.

"After we beat Oklahoma State, Tulsa, TCU, and Baylor we thought we were pretty good," Dicus says. "Our offense was clicking. We were developing an identity. We had an extraordinary sophomore class.

"In our fifth game we scored 29 points, but Texas beat us. They were just better than we were. We regrouped and took them one at a time. The week after Texas we played a North Texas State team that was loaded with talent. They almost beat us. They had four or five guys go to the NFL.

"Then we won at Texas A&M. They were defending conference champs, and it was a tough game. We won the rest of them to tie Texas for the league title. That was a big deal."

Arkansas was 9-1 and as SWC co-champion was invited to play Southeastern Conference champ Georgia in the Sugar Bowl.

THE SCENE

In 1968 there were four bowls that were considered major—the Cotton, Orange, Sugar, and Rose Bowl games. Only eight teams had the privilege of playing on New Year's Day. The Hogs didn't take the invitation to play Georgia for granted.

"We knew it was big playing in the Sugar Bowl," Dicus says. "Georgia was ranked No. 4 in the country with an 8-0-2 record. They had the No. 1 defense in the country. We knew it was big because of the way our coaches treated the preparation. We could tell how excited they were.

"We had worked hard for a chance to play in the Sugar Bowl. Our coaches had a passing game plan based on using me in the slot formation. Georgia had not seen much of that during the season. They relied heavily on man-to-man coverage. They could afford to. Their cornerbacks were exceptional, and their safety, Jake Scott, was the best in the country.

"We had played people who compared to Georgia, but Bill Stanfill, their great tackle, was huge, and Scott was a presence. They had better speed and quickness in the secondary than we anticipated."

Dicus and his teammates enjoyed New Orleans but saved most of their partying until after the game.

"I had been to New Orleans before," he remembers. "It was difficult to be 19 or 20 and get turned loose in that atmosphere. I don't know about Georgia, but our players followed the rules for the most part."

THE GAME
by Chuck Dicus

Early in the game we could tell how difficult it would be to move the ball against Georgia's defense. We weren't making first downs like we expected. The only thing that was working was the short passing game. We tried to pick at them and had some success. Scott wasn't able to get to me. I'd run a five-yard pattern, and Bill would throw it quick. I could make three or four steps downfield before he arrived.

It was 0-0 at the end of the first quarter, but we were driving when the quarter ended. We had reached the Georgia 27-yard line. Scott was playing me man to man, and he was starting to jump on the out route.

On the first play of the second quarter I lined up in the slot on the left and ran 10 yards. Previously I had run an out pattern to the sidelines. I gave Scott a head fake, and he took it. I ran a post up the field and remember thinking, "My gosh, he took the fake, and I'm wide open."

Sometimes the hardest catch is when you are wide open. Bill saw me break and laid it up there for me. I caught it and ran into the end zone. Pictures of the catch show I caught the back half of the ball. It just happened. I can't explain why. Normally you don't get a good grip on the back half and you can lose it. I was glad to hold on.

That turned out to be the only touchdown of the game. We were ahead 10-2 at halftime, and our coaches talked about establishing a running game. We just couldn't run against the Georgia defense. In fact, we only gained 40 yards rushing the entire day. So, we kept using the short passing game and watched Bob White kick field goals. Thank goodness for Bob. He had a great day.

It was a cold day in New Orleans, and the field was a little damp. Footing wasn't perfect. You had to be careful running routes. But I kept running them, and Bill kept hitting me.

It was still 10-2 after three quarters, and I kept thinking any minute Georgia would make a big play. They never gave any signs they were beat. We weren't moving the ball. I kept thinking, "What are we going to do if they get ahead?" I wasn't sure we could score other than field goals.

Once Bob kicked another field goal to make it 13-2 in the fourth quarter, I felt better. Any time we scored I felt better. He kicked another one to make it 16-2, and suddenly the game was over.

We were all happy. It was our first game on national television that year. That was a big deal. People all over the country had seen how good we were. We showed we could beat the best.

Chuck Dicus

They announced the Most Valuable Player award before we went into the locker room. It was an honor to win. When they told me I caught 12 passes, I couldn't believe it. I didn't think it was that many.

Our fans were fantastic that day. Arkansas fans always have amazed me. Normally I didn't pay attention to the stands during a game, but I could sense the excitement in that big, big stadium.

When all was said and done, our defense really won the game. Georgia's defense got all the pregame attention, but our defense recovered five fumbles, intercepted three passes, and stopped Georgia all day.

I'm not sure it all hit me until later. I always have tried to be modest, and I really didn't know how to handle all that attention. During the next two years we were privileged to get a lot of attention, and I was more settled with it.

POSTGAME

The day after the Sugar Bowl both teams attended the horse races in New Orleans.

"They had a big room for us to eat together," Dicus recalls. "When it was time for the first race, I went outside and was standing by a rail when I noticed Jake Scott standing next to me. I introduced myself. He told me he hoped I would be as lucky at the racetrack as I'd been in the football game."

Dicus believes that day changed his life.

"After having a game like I did against Georgia, I had an obligation to perform," he explains. "Fans expected me to be good, and I had to produce. I've been amazed at the things that have happened to me since. I don't feel worthy. All I've tried to do is work hard, show dedication, and value the team over the individual."

Dicus's hard work and dedication paid off in his final two yars as the Hogs had back-to-back 9-2 seasons and he earned All-America honors.

WHAT HAPPENED TO CHUCK DICUS?

Dicus spent three years in the NFL, two with San Diego and one with Pittsburgh. During the offseasons he sold real estate at Hot Springs Village.

"George Billingsley [an ardent supporter of Razorback athletics] helped me get the job at Hot Springs Village," Dicus says. "When my NFL career was over, I called George and he hired me full time."

When Williamson was named head coach at Memphis State, he hired Dicus to coach receivers. He was an assistant coach for three years and then went back to Hot Springs Village.

Later he moved to Little Rock, where he met his wife, Cathy. Then they relocated to Dallas where he worked in the oil and gas business. It was back to Little Rock where he sold real estate before going to work for Stephens, Inc. in 1985.

"I enjoyed my time at Stephens very much," Dicus says. "Then out of the blue Coach Broyles called and asked me if I would be interested in working for the Razorback Foundation. He didn't have to recruit me very hard."

Dicus loves his work for the Razorback Foundation. He's come a long way from visiting the Arkansas team hotel in Dallas. His son Neal, 30, is a computer technician for the Pulaski County sheriff department. His son Charles is a film major at Northwestern, and his son Jonathan is a senior at Belmont.

CHAPTER 10

ANTHONY EUBANKS

Born: December 11, 1974
Hometown: Spiro, Oklahoma
Current Residence: Fayetteville
Occupation: Student
Position: Wide Receiver
Height: 6-2
Weight: 196
Years Lettered: 1994-1997
Accomplishments: Is Arkansas's all-time pass receptions leader with 153 catches during his career; earned 2,440 receiving yards, second-best ever at Arkansas; scored 16 career touchdowns; caught 51 passes for 870 yards and five touchdowns in 1997.
The Game: Arkansas vs. Alabama, September 20, 1997, at Tuscaloosa, Alabama

BACKGROUND

B orn in Fort Smith, Arkansas, Anthony Eubanks moved to Spiro, Oklahoma, when he was young and had a passion for basketball.

"My brother was three years older than I was, and I wanted to be like him," Eubanks confesses. "He loved basketball so I did, too. He was involved in other sports, including football, so I tried them, too."

As a sixth grader he started football, and his first position was fullback. "I was taller than everyone else, and I knew I shouldn't be a fullback," Eubanks explains. "Plus, the fullback doesn't get the ball much. He mostly blocks."

In the ninth grade he was finally moved to wide receiver. It was about that time he began to realize his future would not be in basketball.

"I was playing center on the basketball team because I was the tallest guy on our team," Eubanks says. "But if I would have the opportunity to play basketball in college, I would have to be an outside player.

"When I was in the 10th grade, my coach told me I could get a scholarship playing football. That's when I decided football was my future. I kept playing basketball, but I was better in football."

Michigan State was the first school to send him a recruiting letter. He was an Oklahoma fan and liked Oklahoma State but narrowed his choices to Arkansas and Texas Tech.

"OU was going through some coaching changes," Eubanks recalls. "Their wide receivers coach got fired. When their new coaches came in, I wasn't high on their list, so I visited Arkansas. When I saw the facilities and the way people treated you at Arkansas, I fell in love with it.

"The biggest thing, though, was the chance to play soon. Coach [Danny] Ford was honest. He didn't promise I'd play right away, but he said I'd have a chance.

"It was a nightmare at first. It was a big change coming from a small town like Spiro. At home we weren't big on weights. Practices at Arkansas were intense. In one practice Carl Kidd hit me so hard I threw up. College was like playing with a team of all-stars. Everyone was good. It was intimidating. I told my mom I wasn't ready for college football, but she told me to keep at it.

"I only weighed 172 pounds when I reported and I redshirted. By the spring of my first year I was up to 185, and I played my entire career between 195 and 200. The extra weight made things better for me."

Fitz Hill was the receivers coach at the time, and Eubanks says, "He was like a father to us. He was in our faces. He stayed on us all the time. He told us we would thank him later, and he was right. He encouraged us through the tough times.

"I got discouraged early in the 1994 season. After redshirting the year before, all I was doing was blocking. I wasn't playing as much as I had hoped. Coach Hill told me to wait my turn and everything would work out. He was right. By the middle of the season I was playing more and making some catches."

Eubanks had a terrific spring in 1995 but made one of the biggest mistakes of his career by spending that summer in Spiro.

"I didn't realize how important summer was," he says. "I came back at 210 pounds and wasn't in great shape. Coach Ford was upset with me. It was the last summer I spent at home."

Still, Eubanks had a feeling 1995 would be a good year.

"We had Madre Hill in the backfield, and a good running game opens up the passing game," Eubanks explains. "We had high expectations. We beat Alabama and Auburn and thought we could beat Florida in the SEC championship game. If Madre hadn't been injured against Florida, there's no telling what might have happened."

The Alabama contest was a thriller. The Hogs trailed 19-10 but came from behind to win. Barry Lunney Jr., tossed a touchdown pass to J.J. Meadors with seven seconds remaining to give the Razorbacks a 20-19 victory.

"I was running a route behind J.J. on the touchdown play," Eubanks says. "I was the deep option. When I saw J.J. make the play, I was so excited I felt I had made the catch. I cheered so hard it wore me out. It was one of the highlights of my career.

"J.J. was a good mentor for me. He had the respect of all the receivers as well as everyone on the team. He was a little guy playing well and breaking records. I figured if he could do that well, I could too.

"Tracy Caldwell helped me, too. He was a graduate assistant coach for a while. He put me in the game for the play that became my first touchdown catch. He wanted to see if I could do it. Coach Hill was in the press box, so Tracy put me in."

Lunney, a near-four-year starter was gone after the 1995 season, and the Razorbacks were breaking in a new quarterback. Things never seemed to jell during the entire season.

"Coming off the SEC Western Division championship season our hopes were high," Eubanks says. "But we were out of sync somewhere. Anthony Lucas got hurt in our first game. They were depending on Lucas and me as receivers. When Anthony went down, it was me and a bunch of young guys. They double-teamed me a lot, and we didn't pass as much."

THE SEASON

B y the time the 1997 season kicked off Eubanks was Arkansas's most established receiver. He already had made 102 receptions and had proven to be extremely dependable.

"We had some good young running backs, and we thought we would have a good year," Eubanks says. "Our expectations were high again. Then we lost to SMU in the second game of the year at Shreveport.

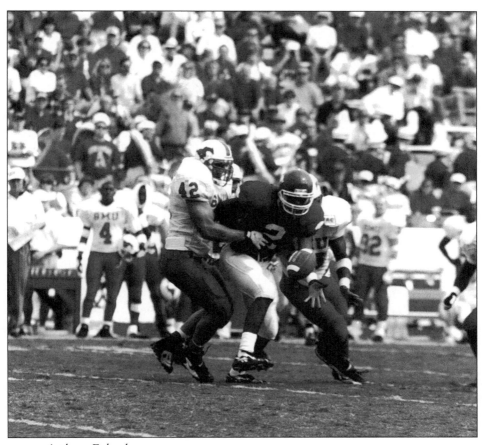

Anthony Eubanks

"Losing to SMU wasn't supposed to happen. The coaches worked us extra hard the next week. We worked a long time on fundamentals. Losing to SMU hit a lot of people hard. We were supposed to win. We showed at Alabama that we had taken the loss to heart and made progress."

THE SCENE

In 1995 Arkansas had defeated Alabama at Tuscaloosa on its way to its first SEC Western Division title. J.J. Meadors cradled a low Barry Lunney Jr. pass in the end zone with seven seconds left to lift the Hogs to a 20-19 win. It was Arkansas's first ever victory over the Crimson Tide.

Arkansas's 4-7 team of 1996 had played Alabama close at Little Rock. Eubanks scored the Hogs' only touchdown, and Alabama was leading just 10-7 until the fourth quarter, when a touchdown ensured a 17-7 Tide win over the Razorbacks.

Eubanks was in his hotel room the night before the 1997 Alabama game when "they showed J.J.'s catch from two years ago. They were still talking about it in Alabama. Their fans didn't think he caught the ball.

"Before the game I had the thought, wouldn't it be something if we won the game the same way we did two years before? We were pumped for the game. We always played well against Alabama. I think part of it was because they had the same color and 'A' that we had. We thought those belonged to us. We didn't like them wearing our colors."

Eubanks didn't know if the Crimson Tide felt the same way about the colors Arkansas wears. He did know how good the Alabama defense was, though.

"They're always good on defense. They are fast. Coach Hill always talked about Alabama's speed. They always played man defense because they didn't need any help. We respected them. We knew we wouldn't put up big numbers and that it would be a dogfight."

THE GAME
by Anthony Eubanks

The first half was strictly a defensive battle. We both scored a field goal in the first quarter, and Alabama kicked a field goal in the second quarter. So, it was 6-3 at the half.

As a wide receiver I don't always know what is going on, but I knew we needed to throw the ball more. That would give us a chance. I was three or four inches taller than their defensive backs. That gave me the opportunity to make plays without them having a chance to stop us.

We mostly ran the ball in the first half. As a receiver you can't get frustrated. You just keep playing. You never know when you will get your opportunity.

As long as the game is close you always have a chance. In fact, I never thought it was any big deal to be behind at halftime. If you were too far behind in the fourth quarter, that's a different story.

In the third quarter we started throwing some. Clint Stoerner scored on a fourth-down quarterback sneak to give us the lead. But Alabama took the lead back in the fourth quarter. We got a big break on the conversion. They were going for two since they were ahead 15-10, but they had 12 men on the field and were penalized. That forced them to kick. They were just ahead by six. That turned out to be very big for us.

I have to admit I was thinking back to 1995 when we trailed by six in the fourth quarter. I remember on our last drive that year we were exhausted. It was probably the most tired I've ever been in a game. On the last couple of plays J.J. and I didn't even make it back to the huddle. We just stayed out wide and got the play from the sideline.

This time we weren't as tired. We were focused. We knew we had to make some plays. We started our last drive from almost the same place as 1995. We were at our own 42. I think we started at the 43 in 1995. Clint hit four passes in a row, but then he got sacked, and we had third and 18 from the Alabama 29.

The play call was Scissors. Michael Snowden and I would run a crossing pattern. When the play was called, I looked at Mark Baker, our tight end, and gave him the touchdown sign. We had run the play before, and it worked every time.

It worked even better than we could have dreamed. Michael and I crossed, and both cornerbacks went with him. I didn't know it at the time. I thought the defensive back was right behind me, so I jumped to make the catch to shield him from the ball. As it turned out, there was no one around. I was all by myself.

I looked around and realized I was only a yard or two away from the spot where J.J. made the catch to win the Alabama game in 1995. I was excited. It was one of the highlights of my career. Catching a game-winning touchdown pass against a team like Alabama is something that only happens once in a lifetime.

There was still 1:45 left, but we knew the game was over. When our defense was in a position like that, they would stop anyone. There was no way we were gonna blow that game.

When we got into the dressing room, everyone was celebrating. They all congratulated me, but I was just doing my job. There were a lot of heroes in that game.

When we got back, J.J. called to congratulate me. We laughed about how the catch came at just about the same place as his two years earlier. I told him at least mine wasn't controversial.

A guy who was at the game took a great picture of the catch. He blew it up to an eight-by-10 and sent it to me. I have it framed. One day I'll show it to my kids. I never had the chance to meet the man who sent it to me. I'd still like to thank him.

POSTGAME

Arkansas started 3-1 but lost six of its last seven games in 1997, and Danny Ford was fired at the conclusion of the year.

"We wanted to go to a bowl game that year and were disappointed we didn't, but I was fortunate to play with a great group of guys, and we enjoyed the experience," Eubanks says.

"We had some great moments. Anthony Lucas and I made 80-yard touchdown receptions on back-to-back plays against LSU. I'll never forget that. I would've liked to have won more, but for some reason, other than 1995, we never totally jelled as a team. When we did, we were very good.

"It was ironic that Coach Ford had recruited me and we came to Arkansas together and left together. I understand the world of college coaching. You have to produce. We only went to one bowl.

"I wish I could have played one more year. I was in Dallas in 1998, but I was cheering on the Razorbacks. They aired it out that year. Coach Ford recruited most of those players, but coach [Houston] Nutt changed the attitude."

WHAT HAPPENED TO ANTHONY EUBANKS?

Eubanks spent the first half of the 1998 season with the Dallas Cowboys. In 1999 he played for Shreveport in a regional football league. Former Razorback assistant coach Mike Bender was the head coach. The league folded after eight or nine games, and Eubanks returned to school.

In 2000 he became the first player signed by the Arkansas Twisters, a new arena league team in Little Rock.

"They made a big deal out of it," Eubanks says. "The man who owned the Twisters also owned the hockey team in Little Rock. He introduced me between periods of a hockey game. A limo drove me right onto the ice, and I came out in a tuxedo."

Eubanks played four years with the Twisters before returning to Fayetteville to complete his degree. He was scheduled to graduate in December 2005. Eight years after his career concluded, he still held the UA record for career catches.

"When I see that I'm still at the top of the list, it gives me chills and goose bumps," Eubanks says. "When I was a freshman I never dreamed I would accomplish anything like that. I thought about transferring early in my career. I'm glad I stayed. It proves hard work pays off."

CHAPTER 11

ROBERT FARRELL

Born: December 13, 1957
Hometown: Little Rock
Current Residence: Springdale
Occupation: President, Specialty Packaging
Position: Wide Receiver
Height: 6-5
Weight: 197
Years Lettered: 1976-1979
Accomplishments: Was an All-Southwest Conference wide receiver in 1979; was part of a senior class that went 30-5-1 during his last three seasons; made 46 career catches for 904 yards and six touchdowns.
The Game: Arkansas vs. Texas A&M, November 12, 1977, at College Station, Texas

BACKGROUND

Growing up in Little Rock, Robert Farrell always wanted to be a Razorback. "In the 1960s and 1970s Arkansas always had great teams in the Southwest Conference and nationally," Farrell explains. "I well remember The Big Shootout against Texas in 1969. I was a paperboy for the *Arkansas Gazette,* and I won a trip to Fayetteville for that game. I sat in the end zone. Arkansas was it for me."

Farrell and Houston Nutt, who became Arkansas's head football coach in December 1997, grew up together and were very close friends.

"I started playing basketball on a team with Houston in the fourth grade. Each of us was playing on three different teams. We played together on the Boys Club team. We traveled the state to play basketball games. Houston's brother, Dickie, was on the team, too.

"Houston's dad and my dad coached our Little League baseball team. They also both coached our first football team, a YMCA team when we were 11 and 12 years old. From eighth grade on we always played together. We were both three-year starters on Little Rock Central's basketball team as well as the quarterback and wide receiver for the football team."

Farrell and Nutt talked about going to the same school, but it wasn't a sure thing they would be college teammates. Nutt deliberated between Arkansas and Alabama. Farrell looked at the Razorbacks, Texas, and Baylor.

"I had played quarterback for two games during our senior year when Houston was hurt," Farrell says. "I loved it. I didn't have a strong arm, though. Texas recruited me as a receiver and kicker. Arkansas and Baylor just wanted me as a receiver.

"Ken Turner, an assistant coach, recruited me for Arkansas. Coach [Frank] Broyles was an icon to all of us growing up in Arkansas. The night before signing day, Coach Broyles was in our home for dinner. That was a big deal. But once I got on campus, I didn't spend much time with him. We were with our position coaches much more than with the head coach."

Farrell's freshman season was 1976. The Razorbacks were coming off a 10-2 season in which they had defeated Georgia in the Cotton Bowl. Many thought the Hogs would win the Southwest Conference championship again. However, the Razorbacks found themselves in trouble early in the season against Tulsa.

"I had played a little in the first two games," Farrell says. "We were behind Tulsa 9-3 in the fourth quarter at Fayetteville. Steve Little had missed some field goals, our receivers dropped some passes, and everything was going bad. I was on the sidelines thinking I wouldn't play. Then I heard Coach Broyles tell Harold Horton, 'Put that tall kid in there!'

"They put me in and threw a pass to me in the end zone. It went right through my arms. I was devastated. We lost 9-3. Four days later I broke my collarbone in practice, and I was out until the last two games."

Following the 1976 season, Broyles resigned as head coach to devote himself to being a full-time athletic director. He had been Arkansas's coach for 19 seasons. The Hogs were surprised, but no one panicked.

"Back then when the coach resigned, players didn't transfer to other schools," Farrell says. "We wondered who in the world could replace Frank Broyles. The first time I heard Lou Holtz's name, I didn't know who he was.

"I'll never forget our first meeting with Coach Holtz. He walked into our old team film room in a three-piece suit with horn-rimmed glasses on. He told us to sit up straight with our backs against the seat and our feet on the ground. He talked about discipline, and it would be his way or Trailways. He even did a magic trick or two.

"He won me over. He was there on a mission. A head coach is hired and fired based on wins. Things have to be done the way a coach wants it. I liked his attitude. I also appreciated the way he reached out to me.

"My mom had colon cancer in the fall. Coach Holtz spent numerous hours talking with me. He took time to be a friend. On the practice field he was the coach, but away from the field he was my friend."

THE SEASON

Few expected much from Arkansas in 1977. The Razorbacks lost their final four games in 1976, and Lou Holtz wasn't exactly a household name at that time. The Hogs were picked sixth in a nine-team league.

"We had great players, but we didn't have confidence," Farrell remembers. "We could play with anyone, but we didn't know it. We had great coaches. It was hard, brutal at times, but from the first fourth-quarter workout all the way through spring we knew we were being prepared to be very good.

"We were cranked going into the season. Coach Holtz made us believe we could do it. Practices were military-like. We had a military togetherness. He emphasized team and depending on each other."

Arkansas blazed to a 4-0 start with lopsided victories over New Mexico State, Oklahoma State, Tulsa, and TCU. The Hogs outscored their first four opponents 160-25. In game five the Razorbacks played superbly but lost 13-9 to unbeaten Texas.

"I've never been a big stat guy, but I knew we should have won the Texas game," Farrell confesses. "Earl Campbell made one big play, and that was the difference. We wanted to go back and do it again. We were mad and irritated.

"After that we took it one game at a time. We got better each week and played to the best of our ability. We were always ready to play."

Robert Farrell

Arkansas beat Houston, Rice, and Baylor by a combined 99-16 to set up a huge showdown at Texas A&M.

THE SCENE

A rkansas was a big-time bowl regular under Broyles but did not go to a bowl in 1976 after finishing 5-5-1. The Razorbacks had played frequently in the Cotton and Sugar Bowl games but never had been to the Orange Bowl.

Orange Bowl scouts attended the Arkansas–Texas A&M game, and Broyles, who had joined ABC television's college football telecasts as its top analyst, had a rare weekend away from a telecast and sat next to the Orange Bowl reps.

All afternoon Broyles was selling the Orange Bowl scouts on the merits of Arkansas, assuring them Razorback fans would travel in large numbers to Miami. Most thought Penn State was headed for the Orange Bowl to play the Big Eight champion, which turned out to be Oklahoma. Although Broyles was doing a masterful sales job, it would mean nothing without a victory over Texas A&M.

"I didn't play against Texas A&M as a freshman," Farrell says. "I was seeing them for the first time. There was something about that big concrete stadium and the Aggie band. That was college football.

"We knew going into the game the stakes were high. I had never been to a bowl game. I'd watched them. Coach Holtz told us the bowls would take care of themselves. We knew the possibilities, but any bowl would have been big to me. We knew if we beat Texas A&M, we would have options."

Farrell became a major figure in those options. He was always regarded as a large target at six foot five, and he had great hands. His speed, though, was never regarded as a major asset.

"I ran 4.6 in the 40 but for some reason was always regarded as slow," Farrell says. "Our other receivers might have been a little faster, but I did have the ability to get open deep.

"We didn't go into the game knowing we would throw the ball deep. We ran the out and up route every day in practice to get our timing down. If the safety came up on the out route, we knew we could exploit any team. Even though I wasn't that fast, I could run the route. All I ever thought about was running a good route, catching the ball, and then running like heck."

THE GAME
by Robert Farrell

Both teams had great kickers. We had Steve Little. They had Tony Franklin. Earlier that year Steve set an NCAA record with a 67-yard field goal against Texas. He was the best kicker I've ever seen.

Both of them kicked field goals early. Then we moved ahead when Ben Cowins scored a touchdown and Steve kicked another field goal. Ben scored another touchdown just before halftime to give us a 20-10 lead.

We were feeling pretty good at halftime. We knew A&M could come back, but we were very confident. No one had scored more than 13 points against us in our first eight games.

A&M came back, though. They had a big fullback named George Woodard who weighed nearly 300 pounds. He was a load. They drove for a touchdown in the third quarter and then kicked a field goal early in the fourth to tie the game.

When you get ahead and the other team comes back on you, it's hard to stem the momentum. Our offense was struggling, but with Coach Holtz we always thought if the game were close, there would be a point where we would take advantage of the defense and make a big play.

In the fourth quarter Coach Holtz called the out and up route twice. The first time the cornerback bit, but our quarterback, Ron Calcagni, threw a slant to Donny Bobo and hit him for a first down. I was open, but Ron didn't see me.

Bobby Duckworth replaced me for a play. On the sideline Coach Holtz turned to me and called the play again. I went into the huddle and told Ron. A year earlier when I dropped that pass against Tulsa, I had no confidence. This time I could feel the confidence.

When the play started, I remember Ron running to his left. I thought he was running the wrong way. It's an easier throw when running to the right. I ran the route and the cornerback broke on the out route. I turned my head like the ball was coming, then planted my left foot, and went deep. The safety took Bobo on a buttonhook, leaving me wide open.

Ron squared his shoulders and threw it. I caught it twice. I was in full stride and caught the back end of the ball. I pulled it in and ran into the end zone for a 58-yard touchdown. After the game Coach Holtz told the reporters that he felt good when he saw me catch the ball with 1:42 left, because he thought I would run out the clock.

Unfortunately I didn't, and even more unfortunately we missed the extra point. In four years Mike Burchfield only had one bad snap on a field goal or extra-point attempt. He rolled the ball back, and Little missed the extra point. We were ahead 26-20, but A&M had plenty of time.

Texas A&M moved the ball on us but for some reason never called time-out. On the last play of the game they threw a pass into the end zone, and

Patrick Martin intercepted it. He was running down the sideline and would have scored, but Monte Kiffin, our defensive coordinator, was so happy he tackled Patrick. The game was already over, but Patrick should have had a 100-yard return, and we should have won 32-20.

That was a real special moment for me. It was my first college touchdown. It came near the end of the game in front of a hostile crowd with a lot on the line. It was like being on an island I was so open. I was either going to make the catch or not. The easiest part of the play was the catch. Texas A&M had a great defense. Our offensive line had to protect, and Ron had to sell the play.

POSTGAME

After celebrating in the dressing room and answering questions from the media, Farrell found himself sitting by backup quarterback Mike Scott on the team bus. That brief ride had a greater impact on his life than the catch against Texas A&M.

"I looked at Mike and said scoring the game-winning touchdown wasn't all that it was cracked up to be," Farrell explains. "I thought it would be bigger. I didn't leave that stadium satisfied. He told me it was big but it wouldn't fill a void in my life. He told me I was trying to fill the void with football, but I needed to fill it with Jesus Christ. That's when Christ became important in my life. People still remember that catch, but it was two guys sitting on a bus that made the difference to me. That's when my priorities changed."

The following week Arkansas defeated SMU and accepted an invitation to the Orange Bowl. The Hogs beat Texas Tech in the regular-season finale and then stunned second-ranked Oklahoma, 31-6, at Miami.

"We were 11-1 and so were Alabama, Notre Dame, and Texas after Notre Dame beat Texas in the Cotton Bowl. We were No. 3 in the final polls, but I still think we were national champions. Sure Notre Dame beat Texas, but they lost to an unranked team that year. Our only loss was by four points to Texas. Since Texas lost in the Cotton Bowl, Oklahoma was next in line for the national championship, and we destroyed them from start to finish in the Orange Bowl.

"I thought the pollsters missed it. Some years there are split national champions. It should have happened that year."

Farrell completed a solid career with two good seasons in 1978 and 1979. He made a play similar to the one he had against Texas A&M to beat Baylor in the 1979 homecoming game.

WHAT HAPPENED TO ROBERT FARRELL?

F arrell gave pro football a try with the Los Angeles Rams. He never was given much of an opportunity and could never figure out why.

"They told me I wasn't good enough," he says. "That's the first time anyone told me that. I ran a 4.6 in the 40 at Arkansas and was timed in 4.58 by the Rams. Jerry Rice never ran the 40 faster than 4.65.

"I was devastated but had set a wedding date for the fall. I worked as a graduate assistant for Coach Holtz, and DeeGee and I were married in September. After the season I was going to Alabama to interview for a coaching position or I could have gone to Seattle, Atlanta, or Los Angeles as a free agent.

"I was wondering what to do when Coach Holtz told me if I could live without coaching I should, because of the sacrifices demanded to be a great coach. It was good advice coming from someone who couldn't live without coaching."

In 1981 Farrell started working for Specialty Packaging and is still with the company, now as president. He and DeeGee have a son, Josh, who lettered for Arkansas's golf team, and a daughter, Paige, who was a state record-setting runner at Springdale High School before becoming a member of Arkansas's women's track squad.

CHAPTER 12

JOE FERGUSON

Born: April 23, 1950
Hometown: Shreveport, Louisiana
Current Residence: Rogers
Occupation: Real Estate Agent
Position: Quarterback
Height: 6-3
Weight: 195
Years Lettered: 1970-1972
Accomplishments: Was All-Southwest Conference in 1971 and MVP of the 1971 Liberty Bowl; completed 327 of his 611 career passes for 4,431 yards and 24 touchdowns; still ranks seventh on the UA career pass yardage list; threw for 345 yards in one game, second best ever by a Razorback and had 31 completions in that game, still a school record; spent 18 years in the National Football League, the longest NFL tenure by any Razorback.
The Game: Arkansas vs. Texas, October 16, 1971, Little Rock, Arkansas

BACKGROUND

Born in Alvin, Texas, Joe Ferguson moved to Shreveport, Louisiana, when he was a baby. He grew up with football and was a skinny quarterback as a freshman at Woodlawn High School.

"We had a good running back that year and should have won state," Ferguson recalls. "We ran a lot and threw a little. We reached the state semifinals."

By the time Ferguson was a junior his team had a decent offensive line.

"We were still a running team," he says. "Our second game of the year was against Airline High School, the No. 1 team in the state. Our coach told me one day that week that he had laid in bed all night realizing we couldn't beat Airline without throwing the ball.

"So we threw the ball and beat them. Then we beat the No. 2 team in the state doing the same thing. We didn't have that much talent, but opponents couldn't stop the passing game. My senior year we were undefeated and won the state championship."

There were no recruiting services during Ferguson's time in high school. He knew he would have a chance to play college football but couldn't believe too many schools were interested in a 150-pound quarterback.

"My coach, A.L. Williams, knew schools would be interested but wanted to protect me from the pressure during the season," Ferguson explains.

"After the state championship game, Coach Williams gave me a box that was absolutely full of letters. I was flabbergasted. There were letters from every major school, Texas, Tennessee, Michigan, and all the rest.

"Charlie Coffey was the first coach to contact me from Arkansas. Then Don Breaux took over. He and my dad would go duck hunting when Don was supposed to be recruiting me.

"Coach Williams helped a lot during recruiting. He told my dad and me that we should narrow the decision to schools that were throwing a lot. There were only about 10 of them at the time. We narrowed it to Arkansas, Alabama, LSU, Florida State, and SMU. I liked Southern Cal, but it was too far away. Darrell Royal called from Texas and told me I could play for them, but they were running the Wishbone.

"I visited Arkansas, Alabama, LSU, and SMU. Bear Bryant came to my house. My mom loved Bear. He came with his state troopers. He told me he hadn't seen me play, but his assistant coaches thought I was pretty good and that was good enough for him to offer me a scholarship. He took us to dinner that night. It was very entertaining. He left a $50 bill for the tip. We didn't have any money when I was growing up, and I was pretty impressed.

"I liked LSU and probably would have gone there, but they were playing two quarterbacks every game. Eventually it was Don Breaux and coach [Frank] Broyles who sold me on Arkansas."

Even in the days of little recruiting news, Arkansas fans knew about Ferguson. Those who did follow recruiting thought he was the top quarterback prospect in the country. Freshmen weren't eligible at the time. As good as the Razorbacks were, Hog supporters could hardly wait to see Ferguson.

"It was great being a freshman in 1969 because of Wilson Matthews. I respected and loved Wilson. We had a great bunch and were close knit. It was much more demanding than high school. Wilson kept us entertained. I wanted to be around him all the time. Billy Laird and Mike Bender were there as coaches, too.

"Even though Bill Montgomery was there, I didn't want to redshirt in 1970. Looking back, I don't know why. I always admired Bill. He was steadfast. I learned a lot from him. I could throw the ball better than he could, but he was better in a lot of ways. It was a senior team, and he deserved to start.

"We won nine games, most of them by lopsided scores, and our sophomore bunch played a lot. We had a great time that year."

THE SEASON

Montgomery was gone after the 1970 season, and Ferguson became the starting quarterback in the spring of 1971. His presence alone made the Razorbacks one of the favorites in the Southwest Conference race.

"A lot was expected from us," Ferguson says. "Our sophomore group had done well the previous season. We had some seniors back, too. We had great coaches. Joe Gibbs, Ray Berry, and Breaux were on the staff. We were always prepared."

Arkansas started with wins over California and Oklahoma State before being stunned 21-20 by Tulsa. The Hogs bounced back with lopsided wins over TCU and Baylor to set up their annual showdown with Texas.

THE SCENE

Texas had won four in a row over the Razorbacks including The Big Shootout of 1969 when the Hogs hosted the Longhorns in Little Rock.

"There was always a different level of preparation when we got ready for Texas," Ferguson says. "There was more intensity. You could even sense it going to class. Other students would kind of leave us alone that week.

"Our coaches were more intent. They knew what playing Texas meant to the people of our state. They also knew what a Texas game at Little Rock was like. I liked playing in Little Rock. I liked the stadium. It kept the noise in better than our stadium at Fayetteville. It was a bowl. Fayetteville had an open south end zone.

"We knew everyone would be there for the Texas game. The crowd was already going nuts when we got there. It was raining, but that didn't keep the fans away.

"During warmups I wondered how the rain would affect our play-calling, but I didn't worry about it. Nothing changes with rain. They weren't going to postpone the game. We threw the ball more than they did. The only concern was their offense's ability to control the ball. As it turned out, it was the other way around."

THE GAME
by Joe Ferguson

Texas returned a punt to our seven-yard line about midway through the first quarter and scored to go ahead. I knew that wouldn't change our game plan. With Coach Breaux we weren't shy about throwing the ball from anywhere on the field. We threw a lot of play action passes and used max protection. We had to throw effectively to set up the run.

We came right back with a 75-yard drive and tied the game on a pass to Bobby Nichols. The rain didn't bother us at all in the first half. We did everything we normally would have.

In the second quarter we drove 94 yards for a touchdown. No one drove 94 yards against Texas. To be honest with you, I can't even remember how we did it. I remember finishing it with a 10-yard run. I didn't run that much, but we had some option in our offense. We would run out of the I formation. I faked the ball to the fullback, and most of the time I would pitch to the tailback. I just ran to keep people honest. For me to run 10 yards I had to be all by myself.

We got the ball back before halftime and had a quick 56-yard drive to a touchdown. Mike Reppond got behind them for a 37-yard touchdown catch. It was a play action with Mike running a post pattern.

Texas always played one-on-one coverage. Texas's whole defensive scheme was to stop the run first. If you could beat them with the pass, that was it. Reppond and Jim Hodge had the speed and experience to beat people. Both could run. Mike had nearly 200 yards (171 on seven catches) in receiving yards that day.

It was exciting in our dressing room at halftime. We were confident. We knew we could handle them. We were ahead 21-7 and were feeling good.

We got more conservative in the second half. It rained harder, we had a lead, and we wanted to protect it. We still threw some, though. Nichols caught another touchdown pass in the fourth quarter after Bill McClard kicked a field goal. Our defense did a great job, and Texas never scored after that first touchdown.

Joe Ferguson

When the game was over, I had never seen people so excited. There were a lot of wet people at War Memorial Stadium, but no one wanted to leave. There were plastic bags covering people everywhere.

People looked at me different after that game. I still remember that day well. So do a lot of people I meet even today. It had great significance for me.

POSTGAME

Two weeks after beating Texas, Ferguson set school records for completions (31) and yards passing (345), but the Hogs lost to Texas A&M at Little Rock. The next week a tie with Rice knocked the Razorbacks out of a tie with Texas for the SWC lead. Wins over SMU and Texas Tech led to an invitation to play Tennessee at the Liberty Bowl.

"We really messed up against Rice," Ferguson says. "That knocked us out of the Cotton Bowl. Getting ready for the Liberty Bowl was really strange. We were in final exams and really couldn't prepare. We didn't practice much at all. We all drove to Memphis the day before the game. I drove my own car. We just gathered in Memphis and then played the game. We should have won. There were some horrible officiating calls. We were robbed."

In 1972 Ferguson was the preseason favorite to win the Heisman Trophy. He was on the cover of all the preseason magazines.

"I never really felt the hype," he says. "It made me work harder. I knew any chance I had to win the Heisman was related to what kind of team we would have. I never thought I was any big-time player. My career was going so quickly, I didn't have much time to think about it.

"Besides, I was concerned when Don Breaux left. He had such an impact on me and our offense. The season turned out to be a fiasco. We were a senior football team, had 11 players drafted by the NFL, but changed the offense during the season. After three or four games we went to the option. That killed us.

"I didn't play in our last game. That was very difficult for me. It took me a long time to get over that, but everything is fine now."

WHAT HAPPENED TO JOE FERGUSON?

As the NFL draft approached, Ferguson's dad was nervous.

"On the day of the first round he wanted to go fishing," Ferguson recalls. "He took a transistor radio with us, but after an hour he was still nervous and we went home.

"They took a lot longer with each round then, but by late in the afternoon I thought I would be drafted on the second day. Then Buffalo called and asked if I was planning on playing in the NFL or in Canada. I hadn't given a thought to Canada. So the Bills took me in the third round."

Ferguson spent 18 years in the NFL, the first 12 with Buffalo, where he is in the Bills' Hall of Fame.

"It was great playing as a rookie," Ferguson says. "I didn't have to carry the load. I could hand the ball to O.J. Simpson. We had some very good teams and made it to the playoffs but never the Super Bowl. I loved the rivalry we had with the Miami Dolphins. It was like Arkansas–Texas. They beat us something like 20 in a row, but in my fourth year we beat them."

As his NFL career began winding down, Ferguson considered coaching. "I had been thinking about coaching all along," he explains. "My first two years out of pro football, I coached at Louisiana Tech where my brother-in-law was head coach. It was in Ruston, close to my family.

"My third year out of football, I didn't coach, and then we moved to northwest Arkansas. Sandy, my wife, didn't want to move. Now she loves it here. I told Coach Broyles I would love to coach at the University of Arkansas if the opportunity ever presented itself."

For two seasons Ferguson served as sideline analyst on Razorback football radio broadcasts from which he says he learned a lot.

Finally Danny Ford hired Ferguson as quarterbacks coach, and he was reunited with Kay Stephenson, who had coached him at Buffalo, when Stephenson became Arkansas's offensive coordinator in 1997.

"That was interesting," Ferguson says. "By the end of the year, we were getting better on offense, but Danny got fired. Houston Nutt came in, and we did well. I got to coach Clint Stoerner, Chadd Jones, and John Rutledge. That was a good group. Our meetings were fun. Stoerner was such a competitor. I enjoyed coaching him. He saved the day on many occasions."

Before coaching at Arkansas, Ferguson had entered the real estate profession at Lindsey and Associates. When he left the Razorbacks, he returned to the real estate profession and worked with quarterbacks at Shiloh Christian High School. He moved to become an assistant coach in Ruston for a year and then moved back to northwest Arkansas to resume his real estate career.

"I enjoy working with young people and would love to coach at Arkansas again some day or in the NFL," Ferguson says.

Ferguson and Sandy have two children. Their daughter, Kristen, does modeling and is a student at Arkansas. Their son, Trey, enrolled as a freshman at Arkansas in the fall of 2005. Ferguson went through a bout with cancer early in 2005 but by June was declared cancer-free.

CHAPTER 13

QUINN GROVEY

Born: July 19, 1968

Hometown: Duncan, Oklahoma

Current Residence: Fayetteville

Occupation: Divisional Human Resources Manager, Home Depot and Sideline Reporter on Razorback Football Radio Broadcasts for the Arkansas Razorback Sports Network

Position: Quarterback

Height: 5-10

Weight: 183

Years Lettered: 1987-1990

Accomplishments: Was All-Southwest Conference in 1988; is the only quarterback ever to start two Cotton Bowl games for Arkansas; set a school record, since broken, for total offense with 6,242 yards, still third best ever by a Razorback; ran for 1,756 yards and 21 touchdowns and passed for 4,496 yards and 29 touchdowns; against Houston in 1989 produced 335 yards (79 rushing, 256 passing) and five touchdowns.

The Game: Arkansas vs. Houston, October 28, 1989, at Little Rock, Arkansas

BACKGROUND

One of the most elusive quarterbacks in Razorback football history was once an offensive lineman. As difficult as it is to believe, Quinn Grovey once blocked for others because his weight wouldn't allow him to play in the backfield.

"I've been playing football since the first grade," Grovey says. "I was a running back on my first team. In the second grade they had weight restrictions and I was big for my age. Before every game I would get on the scale. The other team would always have someone watching. They didn't want me to be eligible to be a running back. I'd be just over the weight to play running back. I'd have to play offensive line again.

"I didn't want to be there. There's not one glorious moment for an offensive lineman at that level. I had to play on the offensive line for the most part of two or three years."

Freedom came when he moved into the sixth grade. With no weight limits, Grovey moved back to running back where he was a terror for three seasons. As a seventh grader he rushed for more than 2,000 yards in six games and appeared in *Sports Illustrated*'s "Faces in the Crowd."

"I was still bigger than most kids my age, and they were afraid to tackle me," Grovey recalls. "As I got older and the defenders got bigger, they looked forward to seeing me coming."

As a ninth grader he was moved to quarterback, a switch he hated at the time.

"I wanted to be the next Wendell Tyler, who was a great running back with the Rams," Grovey says. "I didn't want to be a quarterback. They moved me anyway, and I scored a lot of touchdowns that year. I started liking the position. After my sophomore year when we won the state championship, I really liked the position."

Grovey also liked basketball. In fact, most observers thought he was just as good on the court as he was the football field. As college recruiters started calling, though, he knew he could choose just one sport.

"I got letters and phone calls from just about everybody, but not everyone wanted me as a quarterback," Grovey recalls. "I narrowed my choices to Oklahoma, Oklahoma State, and Arkansas. Our high school offense was the I Formation, and we ran a lot of option and sprint-out pass plays. I threw the ball about 12 to 15 times per game."

Grovey visited all three schools, and his decision was a difficult one because the recruiting process wasn't always easy.

"Ken Hatfield and his staff were genuine in their approach," Grovey explains. "I felt comfortable there. I didn't have to be someone I wasn't.

"It was rough in Duncan. People there didn't take kindly to me looking at a school out of state. But Oklahoma had just won the national championship with Jamel Holloway, who was a freshman, at quarterback. My chances of play-ing the quickest were at Arkansas.

"OSU was in the picture, too. Louis Campbell was an assistant coach there at the time, and I got really attached to him. He almost made me make the worst mistake of my life."

Despite grumblings from his hometown, Grovey chose Arkansas and enrolled in the fall of 1986. He redshirted that year and realized at the time it was best for him.

"I knew I wasn't ready," Grovey says. "I was more of a running quarterback in high school. After 20 or 30 passes in practice, my arm would start hurting. I already had been labeled as a guy who couldn't throw. It was even more appar-ent when the varsity players showed up.

"At first I didn't take things too well, but Sammy Van Dyke, who was a sen-ior running back that year, stopped me one day and told me to quit pouting. He said redshirting was best for me. Greg Thomas was a junior that year. Redshirting would give me more playing time later."

Grovey got plenty of playing time the following season. Thomas struggled with shoulder problems, and Grovey not only started three games, but he relieved Thomas frequently.

"It was like tag team at quarterback," Grovey says. "Greg's shoulder was hurt, and I had a bruised back and strained groin. It was a crazy year. We won nine games but felt bad. Coach Hatfield helped me a lot that year. He kept telling me to hang tough. Coach Hatfield added a great deal to my life."

Arkansas earned a bid to the Liberty Bowl in 1987, and Grovey figured to split time with Thomas. Unfortunately, his love for basketball kept Grovey from being a factor.

"During our break before heading for Memphis, I went to the gym in Duncan to play basketball," Grovey says. "I twisted my ankle and then tried to think what Dean Weber, our trainer, would do. I used my own treatment process and didn't tell anyone.

"I had terrible practices in Memphis. I was concerned about Coach Hatfield still being at Arkansas. There were rumors from the time we lost to Texas that year on. I just wasn't into it.

"Greg played pretty well, but during the times he was struggling, and nor-mally Coach Hatfield would have put me in, he looked at me and just turned away. I started thinking I had a lot of work to do that spring, or I wouldn't be the quarterback.

"I didn't play a down. I wanted to avoid Coach Hatfield after the game so I got on the third bus. He always rode on the first bus. This time, though, he was on bus three. He told me I needed to get a lot stronger and a lot better."

Grovey used the Memphis trip as motivation when he returned to campus. "I wasn't much for weights until then, but after that I was never outworked in the weight room," Grovey explains. "In the spring I told David Lee, our quarterbacks coach, that I was ready to be the quarterback at Arkansas. From that time on I took a totally different approach. They had recruited four or five quarterbacks. I knew I had to get better, and I did."

He earned the starting job in the spring of 1988, but the Hogs had recruited a thrower, Jimmy Williams, from junior college. After an easy win over Pacific in the season opener, the Hogs were struggling the following week against Tulsa. It was a painful day for Grovey.

"We were behind, and I wasn't doing anything," Grovey says. "The fans booed me. It would be third and 10, and Jimmy would come in the game and complete a pass. I'd come back in, and it would be third and seven. Here would come Jimmy in for another completion. The fans kept booing when I would come on the field. It affected me.

"After the game Coach Hatfield told me I was his quarterback. He said rough times were just part of it. The next week we beat Ole Miss, and we took off from there."

The Razorbacks more than took off. They won their first 10 games before suffering a two-point defeat at Miami. As Southwest Conference champions, the Hogs hosted UCLA in the Cotton Bowl.

"Once again we were worried about Coach Hatfield leaving, but this time it was for another job," Grovey recalls. "We thought he might be going to Georgia. As a quarterback I wasn't as worried because now I was firmly entrenched, but I sure didn't want him to go.

"The Cotton Bowl [loss of 17-3] lit a fire for us. We were just happy to be there. The offense forgot to play. From January 2 through the spring and the summer, we worked to get the offense back. We had unfinished business. We knew we had to win conference games to get back to the Cotton Bowl, and that was our goal."

THE SEASON

Arkansas, Texas, Houston, and Texas A&M were all considered SWC contenders in 1989. Held to 42 total yards by UCLA in the Cotton Bowl, Arkansas hired Jack Crowe as offensive coordinator.

"Coach Crowe was a heckuva offensive coordinator," Grovey says. "He can slice and dice a defense and break it down three or four different ways."

Arkansas's offense, strong throughout the Hatfield years, exploded in 1989. With Grovey, James Rouse, and Barry Foster in the backfield and Derek Russell at wide receiver, the Hogs had plenty of weapons.

The Razorbacks roared to a 5-0 start beating Tulsa, Ole Miss, UTEP, TCU, and Texas Tech by the combined score of 175-52. Arkansas had defeated archrival Texas at Austin in 1988, but the Longhorns stunned the Hogs at Fayetteville 24-20.

"For whatever reason, we were always tight when we played Texas," Grovey says. "Our fans wanted to win that game so bad that it affected us. Even when you went to class that week, students were going crazy wanting to win. I still can't believe they beat us that year."

THE SCENE

Suddenly Arkansas's back was against the wall in earning a return trip to the Cotton Bowl, especially with 12th-ranked Houston and Heisman Trophy candidate Andre Ware visiting Little Rock the next week. Arkansas had been ranked seventh nationally before losing to Texas but fell to 18th after the defeat.

"Coach Hatfield and Coach Crowe told us we had to be perfect on offense," Grovey says. "They told us we had to score every time we had the ball in order to win. Our mindset was that all 11 on offense had to execute perfectly on every play.

"That week every practice was like a game for us. We knew we had to win to go back to the Cotton Bowl. Houston had mauled SMU the week before. We knew how good they were. Really, they were better than Texas.

"The night before the game Coach Crowe told us the team with the better quarterback would win the game. I took that as a challenge knowing how good Andre Ware was."

THE GAME
by Quinn Grovey

Prior to the pregame warmups I was throwing some passes on the field when I saw Andre Ware sitting on Houston's bench. He was in street clothes. I went over and told him I thought he would win the Heisman and wished him good luck in that.

That was calming to me. I knew he was a guy battling to win just like I was. I didn't do anything different from any other game from that point on.

When we came out just before kickoff, I could sense the crowd, but once the game started, I didn't notice. During the game I always blocked out the crowd. All I focused on was those 11 Houston defenders. I didn't notice the crowd again until late in the game when we were ahead. I've been told many times since then that the crowd was unbelievable that night.

I have to admit I watched their offense. I was hoping we would stop them early, but they scored on the third play of the game. When they hit us that quickly, I could tell it would be one of those days. We had to get seven with our first possession.

Quinn Grovey

We weren't really a quick striking offense even though we scored a lot of points, but their safety was playing up close, and on our third play we threw a post route to Derek Russell for a touchdown. That set a confidence level for us for the rest of the game. Our offense was in sync all night, and it was just great to play in a game like that.

Houston was very confident, too. They scored again, but we were perfect- ly prepared and drove for the tying touchdown. Houston's offense put a lot of pressure on you, because if you, made a mistake, they'd kill you. Houston scored another touchdown, but we kicked a field goal before the end of the half. We were down 21-17 but didn't feel too bad. The field goal had given us some momentum.

On the first possession of the third quarter Houston drove to our 11-yard line. We knew if they ever got ahead by two scores, it would be difficult to catch them. Kirk Collins, our safety, made a great play for us. He sacked Ware, forced a fumble, and recovered it. That was one of the biggest plays of the game.

Our defense gave up a lot of points that night but played well. In fact, our defense did some great things. You just have to remember Houston had a super, super offense. They were hitting on all cylinders, just like we were.

We drove for a touchdown to take the lead, but they came right back and scored again. We were down 28-24 heading into the fourth quarter.

On the first play of the fourth quarter, Coach Crowe called for another deep pass to Russell. Houston was in the same defense, so we ran it again. The cornerback was playing inside. I threw the ball over the top, and Derek went and got it.

We got the ball back, but I threw the interception and they tied the game with a field goal. At that point we knew we had to take the pressure off our defense. James Rouse and Barry Foster made some great runs with a couple coming on third downs. I hit two passes to Derek, and we reached their three-yard line.

I made a pitch to Rouse, and their cornerback tried to intercept it. When he missed, James went in for the touchdown.

They dropped some passes on their next possession and had to punt. We put together a methodical drive to take time off the clock. Our offensive line was jacked up. They were opening some holes. I scored on an option play. They hit me late after I already was in the end zone. I told them it was time for them to get out of our state.

That made it 45-31. Houston scored on the last play of the game and made a two-point conversion to make the final score 45-39. After the game Ware crossed the field and we hugged each other. He said it was a great game and that our team was on fire.

The night before we played Tennessee in the Cotton Bowl, Andre called me wishing me luck. He said he would trade his Heisman Trophy to be in my position.

I still love that game. It was an electric night. There was a lot on the line. We had lost to Texas, and many thought we couldn't beat Houston. I wish I could go back, sit in the stands and hear what people were saying during the course of the game.

POSTGAME

Arkansas beat Rice and Baylor to set up a showdown at Texas A&M. The winner would go to the Cotton Bowl.

"Coach Hatfield told us it would be 14-0 before A&M knew what hit, and that's exactly what happened," Grovey remembers. "After that it was a dogfight.

"A&M took the lead in the fourth quarter, and in the huddle the players told me to take them to the promised land. We were in A&M territory, but on fourth down I passed to Bill Winston and saw the ball hit the ground. I thought, oh no, we're going to the Sun Bowl. Then I saw a flag on the ground. They had called pass interference. From that point on, in the huddle I'd remind our players we were 17 yards from the Cotton Bowl. Then it would be 12 yards to the Cotton Bowl. We scored and knew we would be back in Dallas."

Grovey was sick the morning of the Cotton Bowl and was throwing up in the dressing room while the rest of the team went through pregame warmups. Nonetheless, he played every down on offense, and the Hogs set a Cotton Bowl record with 31 first downs in a 31-27 loss to Tennessee.

Hatfield left for Clemson shortly after the Cotton Bowl, saddening Grovey and many others.

"He was my man, my coach. We had jelled so well. I was sick that he left."

Crowe remained and became the head coach. But Grovey's final season was difficult.

"I was so used to winning," Grovey confesses. "We started well but fell apart after losing to Ole Miss. Some good things happened that year, though. Our fans were great. We played hard every week, and they respected that. People realized that year that I could throw. We built some great relationships on that team. We were still hard to stop, and we still thought we could win, even to the end of the year."

A victory over SMU in the finale left Arkansas with a 3-8 record.

"I was sad when it ended," Grovey recalls. "Derek Russell and I walked off that field and couldn't believe it was over. Coach Crowe set a team meeting in a couple of weeks, and I knew I wouldn't be a part of it. Football had been so much of my life, and I knew I wouldn't have it anymore. It was sad for me."

WHAT HAPPENED TO QUINN GROVEY?

After flirting briefly with the Canadian Football League, Grovey knew he had to prepare for his future. Former Razorback basketball star Charles Balentine got him an interview with Wal-Mart, and his business career took off. In 1994 he was invited to work out of the corporate office and returned to northwest Arkansas. He's been there ever since.

He left Wal-Mart to work for Home Depot as a divisional human resources manager and has held that position for six years. He also serves as sideline analyst on Razorback football radio broadcasts.

"I love living in northwest Arkansas," Grovey says. "I have great memories, and the people here have been great to me. I love working on the broadcasts. It's an honor to do it. It's not just a job, it's a privilege. I love being part of the program."

Chapter 14

KEN HATFIELD

Born: June 6, 1943
Hometown: Helena
Current Residence: Houston, Texas
Occupation: Head Football Coach, Rice University
Position: Defensive Back
Height: 6-0
Weight: 160
Years Lettered: 1962-1964
Accomplishments: Led the nation in punt returns in 1963 and 1964, averaging 16.7 yards per return in both seasons; still holds Arkansas's records for punt-return yardage in a season with 518 yards in 1964 and in a career with 1,153 yards; averaged 16.01 yards per career return, also a UA mark; had the longest punt return in school history with a 95-yarder against Tulsa in 1963.
The Game: Arkansas vs. Texas, October 17, 1964, at Austin, Texas

BACKGROUND

Ken Hatfield grew up around sports. He played them all—baseball, football, track, and basketball. In his Hatfield's early years, a man named R.C. Kennedy made a huge impact on his life.

"R.C. Kennedy was the physical education director at my elementary school in Texarkana," Hatfield says. "He loved baseball, and I played on his Little League team when I was 10 and 11. He was a great coach and person."

Hatfield liked the competition involved in sports. One day in the town park they had relays for kids in every surrounding area.

"They came from all over," Hatfield says. "I was the second fastest kid there. That was when I realized I had been born with good speed."

When he was in the fifth grade, Texarkana had an event called the Milk Bowl.

"They would pick two players from every Texarkana elementary school in Arkansas and every one in Texas, and we would play against each other. I got picked. You had to buy your own helmet for the game.

"Most of our guys couldn't afford a helmet. In fact, just one of our players had one. All 11 Texas players had helmets. They beat us, but it was a close game. I scored our only touchdown on a quarterback sneak."

As a sixth grader, he didn't wait to be picked. He just showed up and played defensive end. "We lost 7-2, but I scored the two points on a safety," Hatfield recalls.

After that, his family moved to Helena, and Hatfield poured himself into athletics.

"We had great athletes and great town support," he says. "One year they divided the town into two schools, and one of them still won the state championship. Three years later we won the American Legion state championship. Our senior team went 11-1 and only gave up three touchdowns all year."

After scoring 26 touchdowns as a ninth grader, Hatfield received his first recruiting letter during his sophomore season. Ironically it was from Air Force, a school he later coached.

"I already weighed 160 pounds, the same size I was in college," Hatfield recalls. "I hurt my ankle as a junior and didn't play much, but in my senior season we shut out our first seven opponents, and Wilson Matthews recruited Bill Gray, Kay Kaiser King, and me for the Razorbacks.

"The only two schools I considered were Arkansas and West Point. My brother, Dick, was already at Arkansas. Three days before I was supposed to visit Army, I decided I wanted to stay closer to home and chose Arkansas. I wanted to be commissioned a second lieutenant, and I was able to do that with ROTC at Arkansas."

His freshman season, 1961, was a dose of hard reality.

"It was a real downer," Hatfield says. "No one came to the freshman games. I was used to the excitement of Friday night games and being the top dog. The freshmen would play on Friday afternoons. We were undefeated, though. We finished 5-0."

As the Hogs prepared for the 1962 season they were coming off an 8-3 campaign that finished with a trip to the Sugar Bowl. His first glance at the depth chart made him gulp.

"Doug Dickey told me I was going to play quarterback," Hatfield says. "I was sixth team. I didn't have a choice. In those days players went both ways, so the quarterback also played safety.

"Two weeks before our opening game, coach [Frank] Broyles had the first, second, and third teams scrimmage the fourth, fifth, and sixth teams. The score was only 6-0 when we finished, and Coach Broyles was fuming. I got moved to the varsity, and the week of the first game I got a lot of teaching.

"We were playing Oklahoma State at Little Rock in the first game and would spend the night in Hot Springs. Instead of riding the team bus, I rode with Bill Pace, one of our assistant coaches. He coached me all the way down there. The next day they put me in on defense.

"On the first play OSU ran a sweep off-tackle. There was a hole that must have been 20 yards wide, and this 220-pound tailback comes running right at me. I was wondering how in the world I would tackle him, but I didn't have to worry about it. About that time their tight end got under my shoulder and knocked me out. He just killed me. It was the hardest hit I ever took.

"I got to play a little more, and we won the game. Oklahoma State broke two kickoff returns that might have been touchdowns, but I made the tackles. From that point on I got to play quite a bit, especially to rest Billy Moore, our quarterback, on defense."

Arkansas finished the regular season 9-1 and came within a gut-wrenching 7-3 defeat at Texas of going undefeated. The Hogs were beaten by Ole Miss in the Sugar Bowl.

Hatfield thought the Razorbacks would be exceptional in 1963.

"There were 26 of us who had been sophomores in 1962 back, and I thought we would be great. We didn't realize how much we had relied on our seniors the year before. It was cold and dreary all through two-a-days, and we had a hard time getting in condition."

Arkansas went into its last game with a 4-5 record. All five defeats were by seven points or less, including a 17-13 setback against Texas, the eventual national champion.

"Coach Dickey told us we were playing just well enough to look good while getting beat," Hatfield says.

"The 1964 season started the last week of 1963. We were tired of excuses. We practiced hard the week of the Texas Tech game. Then President [John]

Kennedy was killed, and a lot of games were canceled. Texas Tech was already on the way to Fayetteville, so we played the game. We won 27-20.

"Our offseason was hard. We ran hard in Barnhill Arena. We had great workouts. They continued all through the summer. During the summer the seniors divided up the names of the underclassmen, and we wrote them all letters telling them how much we needed them to have a great year in 1964."

THE SEASON

After their high hopes of 1963 were dashed, the Razorbacks weren't among the picks to win the Southwest Conference in 1964. Defending national champion Texas appeared loaded again, and the Hogs were picked no better than fifth by most of the preseason experts.

"We didn't know if we would win a game," Hatfield explains. "We barely won our first four games. We could easily have lost them all. We beat Oklahoma State 14-10, and Tulsa jumped ahead of us 14-0.

"We couldn't stop Jerry Rhome, Tulsa's great quarterback, but they helped us by throwing a halfback pass that was intended to go back to Rhome. Ronnie Caveness intercepted it and ran it back for a touchdown. We won, but it was close.

"The next week Freddie Marshall, our quarterback, was hurt, and Bill Gray filled in for him. TCU was tough, but we were able to win. Bill made a great interception to stop TCU's last drive. We scored late in a 17-6 win over Baylor. So we were 4-0, but we hadn't beaten anybody bad."

THE SCENE

Arkansas–Texas was always huge to Razorback fans. Hatfield thinks the game became important to the Longhorns in 1960.

"Mickey Cissell kicked a field goal to beat Texas at Austin in 1960," Hatfield says. "Arkansas and Texas had always been rivals, but that took it to a higher level. That win gave the people of Arkansas some pride and convinced them they could beat Texas. To Arkansans, it was like whipping the big state of Texas.

"Texas had won 19 games in a row and was ranked No. 1 in the country again. We were the upstarts. We were 4-0 but hadn't dominated anyone. I remember Ernie Koy was a strong dude and a great punter. Opponents had averaged 2.7 yards per return against Texas. In the paper that morning the sportswriter who wrote the game story guaranteed there would be no significant punt returns against Texas that night."

Ken Hatfield

THE GAME
by Ken Hatfield

I t was a great atmosphere in Austin. Our fans were in the end zone, and there were a lot of them. There was a big track around the football field at Texas, and our fans weren't anywhere close to the field. Texas had a great crowd there. They were the No. 1 team in the country. They were very, very good.

Both teams were good defensively. They ran a power sweep early, and I made the tackle downfield. Coach Matthews told me to get closer to the line of scrimmage, and we would stop that play. I did, and we held them.

It was scoreless when they punted to me. I was on our 19-yard line when I caught the ball. I knew right away they had kicked it too far, and I knew we could block them. Jim Lindsey threw the first block. When I went to the wall on the sideline, our whole team was there. I ran right by our bench, and our players knocked down eight of them. Somewhere around the Texas 35 or 40, Jerry Lamb knocked Koy off balance.

I've seen that play on film several times, and I sure look slow, but the play went 81 yards for a touchdown and put us ahead. I remember looking at our fans after scoring. They were ecstatic. So were we. That play gave us great confidence. Our coaches gave us great confidence, too. We sincerely believed we would win the game.

That was all the scoring in the first half. In fact, it was still 7-0 going into the fourth quarter. Texas finally scored early in the fourth quarter to tie the game. We came right back, though, and drove to their 37-yard line, where we had fourth and four.

We made a last-minute decision to punt. My brother, Dick, saw Texas putting its return team in the game. They were substituting seven players. He called set, and we snapped the ball before they got off the field. Texas was penalized five yards, and we had a first down.

After that Bobby Crockett made a great shoestring catch for about 11 yards. Then Freddie Marshall hit him again for a touchdown to put us ahead 14-7.

It was far from over, though. Texas drove the length of the field on its last possession. That's what they did in 1962 to beat us 7-3. We stopped them all night until the end of that 1962 game. They were even driving toward the same end zone. I was thinking, "Please don't let that happen again." Tommy Ford scored with less than a minute left to make it 14-13.

Texas decided to go for two to try to win the game. They took Koy out, and Jim McKenzie, our defensive coordinator, called a timeout. Back then once a player was substituted for, he couldn't come back in the game until the next play. Texas put Hicks Green in Koy's place. That caused us to think they would pass rather than run.

We changed to a wider defense. We knew they wouldn't run without Koy in the game. Sure enough, their quarterback tried to throw a flat pass to Green, but Jim Finch got in his face and made him throw the ball low. With so little time left, we knew the game was over.

The celebration in the locker room was great. Darrell Royal, Texas's great coach, came into our locker room and told us we had beaten a great Texas team. He told us they wouldn't lose again, and if we let up at all, they would win the conference championship. Sure enough, Texas didn't lose again, but neither did we.

POSTGAME

Arkansas shut out its next five opponents. The Razorbacks blanked Wichita State, Texas A&M, Rice, SMU, and Texas Tech to improve to 10-0 for the first time in school history. In fact, the Hogs had not had an unbeaten season since 1909 when Arkansas was 7-0.

"We were very confident in the second half of the season," Hatfield says. "We had just beaten the No. 1 team in the country. The teams we played after that weren't as good, and our defense was real good.

"We were the host team in the Cotton Bowl and were going to play Nebraska. It looked like that would be a magical game when Nebraska was 9-0, but they lost to Oklahoma in their last game to go to 9-1. It was still a great matchup. The only other unbeaten team was Alabama. They were playing Texas in the Orange Bowl."

Arkansas drove 80 yards late in the game for the touchdown that gave the Hogs a 10-7 win over the Huskers.

"After we celebrated the victory, we all watched the Orange Bowl on television," Hatfield remembers. "It doesn't happen much, but we were pulling hard for Texas. When they upset Alabama, we knew we were national champions."

WHAT HAPPENED TO KEN HATFIELD?

After the national championship parade and celebration in Razorback Stadium, Hatfield's attention turned to his future.

"I had always wanted to play in the NFL, but I still weighed 160 pounds, and my shoulder had been knocked out of place. Plus, I was about to go into the Army for my two-year obligation."

He coached high school football for eight weeks before going into the Army. In November he was told he had a choice of being a liaison with the Korean Air Force or serving as an assistant football coach at Army.

"I opted for West Point, and that's where I knew coaching was my calling," Hatfield says. "Football is important in the development of leaders, and I love coaching. I recruited seven states and was an assistant freshman coach for two years."

After his military stint ended, he went to the national coaching convention in New York City looking for a job. He was offered the defensive backfield job at Montana State and asked Dickey, then the head coach at Tennessee, for advice. Dickey told him not to do anything and then created a job for him with the Volunteers.

His first head-coaching job came years later with Air Force. After upsetting Notre Dame and turning Air Force into a winner, he was named head coach at Arkansas in December 1983.

"Returning to Arkansas as head coach was the greatest feeling I can imagine," Hatfield says. "I was most blessed. I knew I could recruit with passion and love for the school. With the support we had, there was every reason for us to be successful.

"We gave it our best effort for six years. When we lost, we hurt more than anyone because we loved the University of Arkansas. In 1988 we were 10-0 and almost 11-0. We dropped an interception in the end zone late in the game that would have prevented Miami's last field goal. Instead they kicked it and beat us 18-16.

"We went to the Cotton Bowl our last two years. I wouldn't trade those six years for anything. To coach at your alma mater is a special blessing."

Hatfield left Arkansas to become head coach at Clemson and is now the head coach at Rice.

"We have great kids here. We don't have a lot of students. Texas will graduate more in one year than Rice will in 10, but we have good people and great coaches to work with."

Hatfield and his wife, Sandy, enjoy the Houston area. They have been married 36 years.

CHAPTER 15

MADRE HILL

Born: January 2, 1976
Hometown: Malvern
Current Residence: Columbia, South Carolina
Occupation: Assistant Football Coach, University of South Carolina
Position: Running Back
Height: 6-1
Weight: 197
Years Lettered: 1994-1995, 1998
Accomplishments: Rushed for 1,387 yards in 1995, a school record that still stands; was All-Southeastern Conference and three times was the SEC offensive player of the week; carried a school record 307 times, including 45 attempts, a single-game UA record, against Auburn; ranks sixth on Arkansas's career rushing list with 2,407 yards.
The Game: Arkansas vs. South Carolina, September 9, 1995, at Fayetteville, Arkansas

BACKGROUND

Born in North Carolina while his father was in the service, Madre Hill spent his early years at Fort Bragg near Fayetteville. His parents moved to Little Rock when he was young and to Malvern when he was in the fourth grade.

Hill's mother hated football and didn't want him to play. His friends started playing when he was in the fifth grade, but it took a cousin to convince Hill's mother to let him play in the sixth grade.

"I wanted to play quarterback," Hill recalls. "To this day I wish I could have played quarterback. I could have been another Michael Vick. The first time I carried the ball I made a great run, and I've been a running back ever since."

Although Hill was faster than just about everyone from the sixth grade on, he never looked at himself as being better than anyone.

"I always thought I had to outwork people to prove myself," Hill says. "It was that way even early in my career. When I played peewee football, they changed the participation rule and it became the Madre Hill rule. They said if a player scored four touchdowns, he couldn't play offense the rest of the game. I would move to defense and return an interception for a touchdown. So they changed the rule again and said if a player scored four touchdowns, he couldn't play anymore in that game. I would score on every play I was given the ball.

"We were undefeated during my ninth grade season, and during my sophomore year I started getting recruiting letters. We were running an offense that wasn't suited for me. We had a fullback and two slotbacks. I had to be facing the defense to be successful. I was never a lateral runner. We changed to the I formation during the season, and we were off and running."

Hill ran and ran his way to every state rushing record. Recruiters flocked to his door, but his main interest was Notre Dame.

"It sounds weird for as long as we lived in Malvern, but many of the people around us were not big Razorback fans. My mom and dad had become Razorback fans, and Arkansas was their first choice for me, but I was a diehard Notre Dame fan. Lou Holtz was the head coach, and it was my dream to go there.

"I liked Florida State and West Virginia, too, and wasn't even planning on visiting Arkansas. I changed my mind when Danny Ford visited our home.

"You have to remember I always had to be challenged. Everyone thought I was good, but I always wanted to be better. I wanted to be the next Walter Payton. In our house Coach Ford told me I was a little thin for the SEC and I would have a hard time rushing for 900 yards in that league.

"When he said that I knew I was going to Arkansas. He challenged me. Once he told me I couldn't do something, I wanted to do it. He couldn't have known it, but it was the right pitch at the right time.

"On my visit he told me Robert Reed, Tyrone Henry, and I would be the keys to this class. He said the other ingredients were there to win a championship. Vincent Bradford, who was from Malvern, showed me around. On Sunday I walked into the coaches' staff meeting, told them I was coming to Arkansas, walked out, and drove home."

As a freshman in 1994 Hill didn't think the SEC was as hard as he had been led to believe.

"I remember J.J. Meadors telling me how tough the SEC was. It didn't seem that hard to me. I was able to do just about anything I wanted to do. Before my injury I was truly blessed. I would tell people what I was going to do before I did it.

"I was talking to one of the team doctors in our training room before playing Vanderbilt in 1995. I told him I would rush for 200 yards. That week I rushed for exactly 200 yards. Later I thought, 'Why don't I do it again?' It seems like if I thought about something, I would do it.

"Anyway, in 1994 Coach Ford wouldn't play me. Every week I asked him and the assistant coaches to give me a chance. I think Coach Ford liked big backs. I wasn't his type of back. Maybe he had to sign me because I was from Arkansas and was so highly recruited.

"When the season was over halfway over and we were losing, they gave me a chance against Mississippi State. I had a long run right off the bat. They put me on the kickoff return team for the first time in our last game of the year against LSU. I ran a kickoff back for a touchdown. I just wanted to play."

THE SEASON

Despite the strong finish to his freshman year, Hill was not a starter at the outset of spring practice. But Oscar Malone and Marius Johnson were injured, and he took nearly every snap at tailback. That was just the break he needed to impress Ford and his staff.

"I thought we would be very good in 1995," Hill says. "I didn't think we would lose a game. Then in the first game of the season SMU kept grabbing my facemask. I thought, okay, if that's how it's going to be, I'll have to step up.

"Late in the game I was about to score a touchdown to put us ahead, and they grabbed my facemask again. It kept me out of the end zone and put the ball on the one. We fumbled on the next play and lost the game.

"The next week Coach Ford ripped into me. He said I wasn't running hard. I think he knew that in a lot of ways the team would go as I went. He used me to motivate everyone. He told me I wasn't running like an SEC-caliber back. He did it in front of the whole team."

Madre Hill

THE SCENE

South Carolina was next on Arkansas's schedule. It was the first SEC game of the young season, and Hill knew the Hogs would be ready.

"It didn't matter who we played, they were gonna get it," Hill says. "We had a quarterback controversy going into the first game of the year. Barry Lunney was the returning starter and was a senior, but they started Robert Reed.

"I didn't care about all that, but I did prefer Lunney. Reed was always trying to be the man, and I was too. He wouldn't hand me the ball. Barry did what our offense called for. He wanted to win. He gave me the opportunity to touch the ball. Robert quit after the SMU game. That was okay. We were ready to go.

"I always read the paper to look for motivation. I wanted to lead the SEC in rushing that year. Robert Edwards of Georgia had scored five touchdowns the same week we lost to SMU. I was thinking to myself that I needed to score six touchdowns.

"First priority is always winning, but after that I wanted to outdo the other backs in the SEC. I watched Mo Williams of Kentucky all year. I'd look to see what he did to see what I had to beat. If someone ever rushed for 300 yards, I'd have to rush for 301. So, since Robert Edwards had scored five touchdowns, I wanted to beat him."

THE GAME
by Madre Hill

I scored the first touchdown of the game on a short run over the left side. I appreciated the holes the line would open up, but I never looked at who was playing on the offensive line. That even dated back to high school. The only thing that mattered to me was running. I figured the line would do its part, and it was up to me to do mine. God gave me the ability to run. That was my job.

I say that because late in the second quarter, they put the entire second-team offensive line in the game with us backed up to our own five. I didn't even know it at the time. I was just focusing on running. We drove 95 yards, and I dove over the pile for the touchdown.

When we came out for the second half, I was standing next to Virgil Knight, our strength coach. He asked me how I felt, and I said pretty good. The reason he asked was because I have real bad asthma. I could be a poster child for bad asthma attacks. The worst time of the game for me was always the beginning.

I would just about die in the warmups. I'd be excited, going full speed and thinking about what I needed to do. That always triggered asthma attacks. I could barely breathe.

The longer the game went, the stronger I would get. I could breathe better. I was usually twice as good in the fourth quarter as the first. So I was glad to feel better for that second half.

I scored a touchdown in the third quarter and got into a pattern. By the fourth quarter we were winning, and everything was better. Since we were ahead, I thought I had to do as well as Edwards. I saw him in the Atlanta airport once and told him how his five touchdowns had motivated me.

I scored two touchdowns in the fourth quarter and was excited. Coach Knight was my buddy, and I remember going to the sidelines and telling him how excited I was to score five touchdowns. He asked me why didn't I get six? That became my goal. I wish he would have said seven. I would have broken the SEC record instead of tying it.

The sixth touchdown started on the right side. I hit off-tackle, and the hole opened wide. I knew if I could get through the hole, I was gone. I had never been caught from behind. Before my first knee surgery I even shocked myself at how fast I was.

In fact, I never ran a 40-yard dash when totally healthy. My best time was 4.3 with a sore Achilles. I probably could have run 4.29 when I was at my best.

It was great to get that sixth touchdown. It was a 68-yard play. I thought about beating Edwards. At that point I didn't think we would lose another game.

POSTGAME

In fact, Arkansas won eight of its next nine games, losing only to Payton Manning-led Tennessee in a 49-31 shootout. Hill rushed for more than 100 yards in the first quarter of the Hogs' first ever win at Alabama, and two weeks later had his 200-yard effort at Vanderbilt.

Hill's 70-yard touchdown run was the difference in a 13-6 victory over Ole Miss, and he had a school-record 45 carries as the Hogs beat Auburn at Little Rock. The Razorbacks wrapped up their first ever SEC Western Division title with a win over Mississippi State.

Arkansas was set to meet Eastern Division winner Florida in the SEC championship game at Atlanta. It was a game that forever altered Hill's career as a running back.

"Before the game I was thinking Coach Ford didn't give me enough public praise. If I had rushed for over 1,300 yards at any other school, they would be promoting me for the Heisman. That wasn't happening at Arkansas.

"I was talking to one of our academic advisers and wondered what would happen if I didn't play in that SEC championship Game. I wish I had never said that. Remember, I always believed if I thought something, it would happen."

Arkansas took the early lead with a field goal, but on the scoring drive Hill injured his knee. As it turned out he tore his ACL, causing him to miss the final three quarters and the bowl game against North Carolina. The Hogs lost both games.

He rehabbed furiously and tried to come back too soon.

"Dean Weber, our trainer, tried to get me to wear a knee brace. I wouldn't do it."

Sure enough, he suffered another knee injury. He didn't play again until 1998. By that time Houston Nutt had replaced Ford as head coach.

"I think Coach Ford felt the pressure to get me back on the field," Hill says. "He knew I was a big part of the offense, and he was under pressure to win. Coach Nutt was totally different. He took the pressure off me. It was like a total new start with him.

"I enjoyed my season with Coach Nutt. It's amazing I did anything. I came back out of shape. My knee was okay, but I had gained 18 pounds. I wasn't practicing, just rehabbing. Now, the same injury I had isn't that big a deal, but back then it took longer to deal with."

Hill left Arkansas proud of the record he set in 1995 but hopeful someone would break it soon.

"I hope Arkansas recruits a back that wants to break the record. That record needs to be broken. A record shouldn't stand 30 years. I don't want to be the top brick. I just want to be a foundation that they keep building on."

WHAT HAPPENED TO MADRE HILL?

Despite his knee injuries Hill had a burning desire to play in the NFL. It was another challenge.

"After two knee surgeries, most people didn't think I would make it in the NFL," Hill says. "I was drafted by the Browns and made a lot of friends there. After two years they sent me to Europe to play, and the coaching staff was fired while I was gone. Butch Davis didn't know me, so I ended up in San Diego.

"LaDainian Tomlinson was holding out, and they told me they would keep me if he didn't sign. When he signed late, I got cut. So I went to the Raiders. If you don't have speed, Al Davis doesn't want you. I ran a 4.38 in the 40 on grass, and he signed me on the spot.

"In 2003 I had a great preseason. Al Davis told me I would make the team, but then said it would come down to Tyrone Wheatley or me. They were paying him more money. They tried to trade Tyrone and then tried to trade me, but it didn't work out, so they cut me."

The Raiders tried to re-sign Hill but his wife, Jennifer, was having complications in her first pregnancy. Hill put his family first and turned down offers from Tampa Bay and Seattle as well as the Raiders. When his son, Madre Jr., was born, Hill decided to give coaching a try.

There were no vacancies on Arkansas's coaching staff, so Hill worked as a graduate assistant in the weight room for Nutt in 2004. Following the season he got a call from new South Carolina coach Steve Spurrier, who hired him as running backs coach.

"Now I just want to help other players achieve their goals."

CHAPTER 16

MATT JONES

Born: April 22, 1983
Hometown: Fort Smith
Current Residence: Jacksonville, Florida
Occupation: Player, National Football League
Position: Quarterback
Height: 6-6
Weight: 237
Years Lettered: 2001-2004
Accomplishments: Graduated as Arkansas's career leader in total offense with 8,394 yards and touchdown responsibility with 77 touchdowns rushing and passing; ranks second on the UA career passing list with 5,837 yards and sixth in career rushing yards with 2,537; ran for more yards than any quarterback in Southeastern Conference history; was drafted in the first round by Jacksonville in the spring of 2005.
The Game: Arkansas vs. Ole Miss, November 3, 2001, Oxford, Mississippi

BACKGROUND

G rowing up Matt Jones thought he would somehow play major league base-ball, pro football, and pro basketball at the same time. He began playing baseball when he was four years old, basketball when he was six, and football when he entered the seventh grade.

His father, Steve, was a football coach so Jones was around the sport long before he played it. Once his friends started playing football, he joined them. He was a quarterback from the beginning.

He later traded baseball for track, and as a high school sophomore moved to wide receiver at Van Buren. He moved back to quarterback for his junior season and then switched to Fort Smith Northside where he quarterbacked his senior campaign. He continued to play basketball, and one conference coach labeled him the best basketball player in his league since Corliss Williamson, a standout member of Arkansas's 1994 national championship team.

Because Jones didn't grow up as an ardent follower of Razorback football, he wasn't an automatic recruit for Arkansas. In fact, Oklahoma was strongly in the hunt throughout the recruiting process.

"Arkansas was one of the few schools that would allow me to play football and basketball," Jones says. "Oklahoma and Miami also said I could play both. Arkansas and Oklahoma were both recruiting me as a quarterback. Miami looked at me as an athlete and projected me at wide receiver.

"I narrowed it to Arkansas and Oklahoma and nearly committed to OU. In fact, I told my dad I wanted to commit to Oklahoma and he asked me to wait before making any announcement. In the end, I thought Arkansas would be the best fit because I'm from here and I could play both sports. Playing both sports was a big thing to me."

THE SEASON

A t first it looked like Jones would redshirt in 2001, his true freshman year at Fayetteville.

"I redshirted for the first three games. I guess the plan was to redshirt me all year. But we were having trouble moving the ball, and the coaches could see I had ability. They thought I could help the offense."

Jones's first experience came at Georgia where the Razorbacks lost, falling to 1-3. Jones played wide receiver but didn't make a catch.

"The coaches told me I would play wide receiver as a freshman, then move to quarterback in the spring. I'd played a year as a wide receiver in high school so that was okay with me."

Plans changed the following week when he quarterbacked late in a game against Weber State and had an electric 59-yard run for a touchdown.

Matt Jones

"The touchdown run against Weber State turned out to be one of the most significant plays of my career," Jones says. "After that I played some wide receiver but a lot more at quarterback.

Ninth-ranked South Carolina, coached by former Razorback head coach Lou Holtz, visited Little Rock the next weekend. Jones became more of a factor in the game plan.

"I was a wide receiver in the first half and made a couple catches," he says. "In the second half they inserted me at quarterback, mostly on third-down plays. I would run for the first down, then Zac Clark would come back in."

Arkansas upset the Gamecocks and then drilled Auburn at Fayetteville. Clark continued to start, but Jones received more playing time at quarterback.

"Zac was the starter, and that was fine with me," Jones says. "I was playing a lot. I was only a freshman, and we were winning. You can never go wrong when the team is winning. Everything is good then. If we were losing, that would have been different."

Arkansas had won three in a row to improve to 4-3.

THE SCENE

Razorback fans were increasingly curious about Jones, a long-striding quarterback who was different than any signal caller in Arkansas history. They would learn much more about him when the Hogs visited Ole Miss. Although the Razorbacks had won four games, they had yet to win on the road. They had been beaten at Alabama and Georgia and hadn't won at Oxford since becoming an SEC member in 1992.

"We knew we needed a win to keep our momentum," Jones says. "We hadn't won on the road yet, so we knew Ole Miss was a big game. I don't remember much about practice that week, but we knew we were good enough to beat them. We all knew what a great quarterback Eli Manning was, but we were confident and excited to play.

"Since we hadn't won on the road and the game was at night, coach [Houston] Nutt had us take a shower at the stadium when we got there. That's what I remember most about the pregame."

THE GAME
by Matt Jones

Zac started the game at quarterback, and I played some at wide receiver in the first three quarters. I was open a couple of times, but they didn't throw it to me. Who knows, had they thrown to me we might have won the game in regulation. As it turned out, the first half was mostly defense. Ole Miss scored, and then Cedric Cobbs scored a touchdown for us to make it 7-7 at halftime. Both teams kicked field goals in the third quarter.

They put me in at quarterback in the fourth quarter, and we drove to a touchdown. Mark Pierce scored on a short run. We thought we were in pretty good shape, but Manning hit a touchdown pass to tie the game and send it into overtime.

I had been playing the entire fourth quarter, and Ole Miss couldn't stop our running game, so they left me in during the overtime periods to see if I could continue making plays. Even in the overtimes they never really stopped us.

In the first overtime we had fourth and one at the 16. Cobbs was such a strong runner the coaches wanted him to carry for the first down. He ran to the left side and went all the way for a touchdown. We kicked the extra point and then hoped our defense would stop them.

Ole Miss came right back and scored. Manning threw another touchdown pass to tie the game. They had the ball first in the second overtime and had a turnover. We were excited then. We had a good kicker in Brennan O'Donohoe, so we wanted to give him a chance to win the game.

We didn't want to throw an interception so we kept the ball on the ground. We figured we could make a 30-yard field goal. Unfortunately, we didn't, and the game was still tied.

On the first play of the third overtime we called a bootleg. When I turned the corner, I couldn't believe how open I was. No one ever came close all the way to the end zone. At that point we had to start going for two. We didn't make it, so all we could do was pull for our defense.

We didn't keep Ole Miss from scoring a touchdown, but we stopped the two-point play. Then Ole Miss scored first in the fourth overtime to take the lead back. They missed the conversion again, giving us a chance to win.

On the second play I rolled to the right, and George Wilson broke off his route and went with me just like he is supposed to in a scramble drill. He was wide open for the touchdown. But we missed the conversion again.

In the fifth overtime I scored on an eight-yard run. We got a little lucky there. My knee hit the ground before I got in, but they gave us the touchdown. Then we missed the two-point try again. So did Ole Miss. Manning threw a touchdown pass, but they didn't get the conversion.

By the sixth overtime it was obvious both defenses were tired. Neither team could stop the other. Ole Miss had the ball first. They scored and made the two-point try. We went to our running game. Pierce scored the touchdown on a short run. On the two-point play I was scrambling and saw Jason Peters, our tight end, in the back of the end zone. I threw it up there for him, and he made a great catch.

Once we got to the seventh overtime I was ready to get it over with. I was tired. I told coach John Thompson, our defensive coordinator, to stop them so we could go home. We moved the ball on the ground again, and Pierce had another short touchdown run. On the conversion we were looking for Peters again. DeCori Birmingham was supposed to go to the outside, but he ran to an open area, and I threw it to him. I was hoping that would be good enough to win.

Ole Miss scored, but on the two-point play Jermaine Petty tackled the receiver short of the goal line. Finally, we had won. We were thrilled to win, but everyone was exhausted. I was ready to get on the plane and go home. I didn't even care if we changed clothes. I was tired.

Two years later we played another seven-overtime game at Kentucky. I was just as tired that night. Those two nights are as tired as I've ever been.

That win really got us going. We won six in a row and played Oklahoma in the Cotton Bowl. It was a great win for our program. It's a game I'll always remember.

POSTGAME

Jones finished his freshman season with a single-season UA record for rushing yards by a quarterback even though he didn't play in the first three games. His popularity soared, and for four years he was almost like a rock star in Arkansas.

"Since I hadn't followed the Razorbacks that closely, I didn't realize how big it was," Jones says. "My favorites growing up were Ward at Florida State and Frazier at Nebraska. They were running quarterbacks. I knew Arkansas football was big, but it was a lot bigger than I thought."

As a sophomore Jones didn't start much, but there was no doubt he was the quarterback as he helped lead the Hogs to a spot in the SEC championship Game.

"Winning the Western Division was the highlight of my sophomore season," he says. "I wasn't having a very good game against LSU, but we got the ball back at the end, and I threw a touchdown pass to DeCori with just a few seconds left. He made a great catch. That was probably the biggest play of my career. It was one of the biggest plays in school history because it gave us a championship.

"I wish we would have won against Georgia in the SEC championship Game and played in a BCS game. That would have made beating LSU that much sweeter."

By his junior season Jones was a folk hero. When the Razorbacks beat Texas at Austin in the second game of the season, he moved into legendary status.

"Winning at Texas was a lot of fun. Winning there and winning at Alabama were the highlights of my junior year. We got off to a great start. The overtime win at Kentucky was exciting, too."

The Razorbacks vaulted to seventh in the national polls after starting 4-0. The win at Texas was considered a major upset, and the Hogs overcame a three-touchdown deficit to win in two overtimes at Alabama. Jones directed the Razorbacks to six touchdowns and a field goal in the seven-overtime win at Kentucky.

Adding a six-overtime loss at Tennessee during Jones's sophomore season, Jones took every snap for 22 overtimes during his career as a Razorback. The two seven-overtime games were the longest in NCAA history at the time, and the six-overtime game was next. No player has come close to the number of overtimes quarterbacked by Jones.

"That's a record that might stand for a long, long time," Jones says. "It's like Cal Ripken's record for longevity. Twenty-two overtime periods are an awful lot. I can't imagine that happening again."

Gutted by graduation and early departures for the NFL, Arkansas had just one returning on offense in 2004—Jones. He did his best, but the Hogs finished 5-6 with all but one loss coming against a bowl-bound team.

"I'll have good memories of my senior season, but mostly it was a season of what ifs," says Jones. "I fumbled the ball late against Texas. I wish I would have held the ball and seen if we could make a field goal to win that game. We fell behind early at The Swamp, but I thought we were going to come back and beat Florida. It just didn't happen. We had a very close loss to Georgia. We were close but had too many what-ifs."

Jones did not play basketball during his senior season. He played as a freshman, skipped his sophomore season to let his shoulder heal, and then played again as a junior. He played for coach Nolan Richardson the first time and then for Stan Heath.

"I really enjoyed playing basketball," Jones says. "There aren't many athletes who get to play both football and basketball in college because both are year-round sports. I really had a lot of fun. I had a dunk early in my freshman year, and it was great playing in the SEC Tournament in two different seasons."

WHAT HAPPENED TO MATT JONES?

In the spring of 2005 Jones wowed NFL scouts with a 40-yard dash time of 4.4, incredible for a player his size. It led to his selection by the Jacksonville Jaguars with the 21st pick in the first round of the NFL draft.

"Ever since I was little I've wanted to play professional sports," Jones says. "I just didn't know what sport it would be. It's a dream to play in the NFL, and I'm ready to give it a shot."

Looking back, though, he's glad he chose the Razorbacks.

"I wouldn't trade the experience I had at Arkansas for anything. I had a lot of fun. Certainly the Ole Miss game is one I will never forget."

CHAPTER 17

ANTHONY LUCAS

Born: November 20, 1976
Hometown: Tallulah, Louisiana
Current Residence: Little Rock
Occupation: Executive Director, LifeChamps
Position: Wide Receiver
Height: 6-3
Weight: 196
Years Lettered: 1995, 1997-1999
Accomplishments: Was All-SEC freshman team, 1995, second-team All-SEC, 1998, first-team All-SEC, 1999; set school single-season (1,004 yards) and career (2,879 yards) records for receiving yards as well as UA season (10) and career (23) standards for receiving touchdowns; averaged 21 yards per career reception.
The Game: Arkansas vs. Kentucky, October 3, 1998, at Little Rock, Arkansas

BACKGROUND

A lthough Tallulah, Louisiana, had just 400 students in its entire high school, Anthony Lucas was one of many talented athletes. He played football, basketball, and baseball and began receiving recruiting letters during his junior season.

"I got a lot of letters," Lucas recalls. "Being recruited was a great experience. We got nonstop phone calls from coaches. It was tough to choose. I was hearing from schools like Miami, Tennessee, and Auburn. I did a lot of praying and consulting with my family.

"I committed to one school, Nevada–Las Vegas; signed with another school, Louisiana Tech; and enrolled at another school, Arkansas. When my ACT score wasn't high enough, my national letter wasn't valid. Coach Fitz Hill had been recruiting me for Arkansas, and he stayed with me. The other big-name schools shied away because of my test score."

Lucas and his friend Marvin Caston, another Louisiana native, enrolled in the fall of 1994, but they weren't eligible. They did everything together, and by the end of the first semester, both had gained eligibility.

"Marvin and I encouraged each other," Lucas says. "It was disappointing not to play, but it was a great learning experience. We had a full semester to observe and learn. We were on scholarship in the spring and that was great."

It didn't take the Hogs long to figure out Lucas was a jewel. Hill was persistent in recruiting Lucas, because he knew Lucas could make an impact.

"Before the 1995 season Coach Hill told me if I would prove I could play, they would throw me in the fire early," Lucas says. "I got an opportunity. I was lacking as a blocker, and I ran the wrong routes at times, but my freshman year set the tempo for my career."

The 1995 Razorbacks lost their opener at SMU but battered South Carolina in game No. 2. They hadn't defeated Alabama before or since joining the Southeastern Conference, but Lucas played a key role in the Hogs' win at Tuscaloosa.

"We had a fourth-and-16, and I was the second or third option for our quarterback, Barry Lunney, just as I was for most of the year," Lucas remembers. "I was able to get open and make the catch, and we drove for the winning touchdown. It was great to be a part of that, but the most special catch of my freshman year came against Memphis when I scored my first touchdown. That gave me a feel for college football and made me believe I could play at this level."

The Hogs won the SEC Western Division, and Lucas scored Arkansas's only touchdown in a Carquest Bowl defeat against North Carolina. Named to the All-SEC freshman team, he was primed and ready for a big year in 1996.

"I had worked hard and was expecting a tremendous season when I got hit against SMU and was out for the year," Lucas says. "I came back later and practiced with the varsity as well as the scout squad. I wanted to prove to the coaching staff how badly I wanted to improve. Jerry Rice was my idol. He played hard on every play. I wanted to do the same, whether I was practicing with the varsity or giving a good look to the defense as a member of the scout team."

Lucas bounced back with a solid season in 1997. He caught an 80-yard touchdown pass against LSU but knew before the game something was up. He went outside the dressing room and saw head coach Danny Ford crying. He knew then it would be Ford's last game as coach. After finishing 4-7 in three of his last four years at the helm, Ford was fired.

"It was good playing for Coach Ford," Lucas says. "I respect him and thank him for recruiting me, but it was obvious the program needed a change. We didn't know what to expect with coach [Houston] Nutt, but the first time he met with us was one of the greatest feelings I've ever had. He brought so much to the table.

"In our first meeting, the first thing he noticed was how all the white players sat on one side of the room and all the black players sat on the other side of the room. He said he never wanted to see that again and had us sit mixed together. The things he said and expected of us were unbelievable. We had just finished the season, but we were all ready to play the next day."

Even spring practice was fun according to Lucas, and the Razorbacks couldn't wait for the 1998 season.

THE SEASON

During the preseason there was an energized, confident attitude as the Razorbacks prepared for their first campaign under Houston Nutt.

"We knew the kind of team we could be, but we had to believe in ourselves," Lucas recalls. "Coach Ford was down on us. Coach Nutt got us to believe we could be a good team. When the season started, I was getting the ball, we were winning, and we enjoyed a great turnaround. I love Coach Ford, but Coach Nutt was a welcome change.

"We even enjoyed practice. Coach Nutt was a leader, a great coach, and a great person. He believes in the word *family*, and that's what our team became. We were a family. That was a big part of our season."

The rest of the SEC was nonplussed by the hiring of Nutt. Arkansas was picked fifth or sixth in the Western Division in all the preseason polls. However, the Hogs had a solid senior class and were loaded with quality juniors like Lucas, Clint Stoerner, Kenoy Kennedy, David Barrett, and others.

Arkansas defeated Louisiana–Lafayette in the opener before meeting SMU at Little Rock. The Mustangs had defeated the Razorbacks three years in a row. Nutt recalls being asked at every Razorback Club meeting if the Hogs could just beat SMU.

Nutt's team sent an early warning to the SEC with a 44-17 victory, but the message didn't compare to the one sent a week later. Ranked 23rd nationally, Alabama suffered a 42-6 setback against the Razorbacks at Fayetteville. Suddenly, the program had been revived.

As the Razorbacks started quickly, confidence was building. Arkansas was being noticed outside the SEC. Was Houston Nutt for real?

THE SCENE

Just as Nutt had revived Arkansas's program, Hal Mumme brought a nearly unstoppable passing attack to Kentucky. The Wildcats had their best team in years when they came to Little Rock for the fourth game of the season. Quarterback Tim Couch was a Heisman Trophy candidate and projected as a first-round draft pick.

"Because Kentucky had Tim Couch and they were winning, we knew it would be a big game in Little Rock," Lucas says. "Coach Nutt and our whole staff let us know how big it was. Coach Hill had us ready. I was sure glad Coach Nutt kept Coach Hill on the staff. That meant a lot to the receivers.

"We were focused. We had won our first three games, and the confidence was building. Alabama was good, but this was our first big test. We didn't want to lose in Little Rock. We love playing there. The fans there are awesome. They are close to the field. I wish I could have played in Razorback Stadium after it was expanded. That's awesome, too.

"At Little Rock the fans are right on top of you. They get loud. As a player, you have to calm down to play there because you can get too excited. We're *the* team of the state. When we get off that bus and walk through the crowd to the dressing room, it's very exciting. When the fans reach out and touch you, it makes you want to do everything you can to win for them.

"While we wanted to win for the fans, we didn't want to let Coach Nutt down. He changed the whole program. Everyone was excited again. We didn't want to let the state down, either."

Starved for good football again after watching the Razorbacks go 4-7 in three of the previous four years, Arkansas fans were hyped for the Kentucky game. There was an electricity at War Memorial Stadium that hadn't been there in a while. Everyone, including Kentucky, was ready.

Anthony Lucas

THE GAME
by Anthony Lucas

As confident as we were after beating Alabama, Kentucky was just as confident. They had Tim Couch at quarterback, and he was a Heisman Trophy candidate. Really, Kentucky hadn't been that good until Couch got there. He was really good, and they had good receivers, too.

Both teams scored touchdowns in the first quarter, but that didn't bother us. We knew Kentucky would score some points, but we thought we would, too. Then they scored again, and we were behind by a touchdown at halftime. Again, we weren't going to panic or anything, but we were a little surprised to be behind. We were also surprised we'd only scored one touchdown.

We'd scored 42 points against Alabama, but a lot of those came in the second half. We thought Alabama's defense was better than Kentucky's, but you never would have known it by the way they stopped us in the first half. We knew we would score in the second half.

What happened, though, was Kentucky scored again. Now they were ahead by two touchdowns. But they missed the extra point. It didn't seem like a big deal at the time, but it sure helped us later. Our fans were quiet. They were trying to help us, but they were as surprised as we were.

Our kicker, Todd Latourette got us back in the game. He made two field goals in the third quarter to get us within seven. Because Kentucky had missed that extra point, we knew a touchdown would tie the game.

Just when we thought we were in good shape, it looked like Kentucky would score again. Couch was hitting his receivers and hadn't made a mistake all night. They were close to our 30-yard line, and we weren't sure we could come back if they took a two-touchdown lead again.

I remember watching David Barrett break on the ball when Couch threw it. I don't think Couch saw him. David intercepted the pass and took it the other way. We were jumping up and down on the sideline when David made the interception. I still don't see how they caught him. He is so fast. Once we made that interception, we knew we would win the game. I was so excited I almost forgot to grab my helmet before going back in.

The interception gave us great field position, but we got called for offensive pass interference and had a long third-down situation. But Kentucky got called for defensive pass interference to give us a first down again.

On the play after the interference, Clint called a double slant in the huddle. At the line of scrimmage he checked off to a slant. I split out a little farther on that call. I was determined to make a play.

I ran the route, and Clint put the ball right on the money. I wasn't going to be stopped short of the goal line. I got popped pretty good as I caught the ball. I stretched toward the end zone with two guys on me. They thought they had kept me out, but somehow I got into the end zone.

We were excited. That touchdown tied the game, and we knew we would win. We wanted to prove we were better than Kentucky and that we were a very good team. We didn't want to let anyone in Arkansas down.

Unfortunately for me, though, I got hit on the thigh with a helmet on the play. My thigh stiffened up and really hurt. I wanted to play, but Coach Hill always told us if we couldn't give our all, don't go in.

I tried to be a good cheerleader, but it was hard not going back with the game tied. I still knew we would win. We got the ball back, had a great drive, and Clint hit Hubert Loudermilk for the go-ahead touchdown.

As much as I wanted to be in the game, I was happy for Hubert. He had been kind of down since he hadn't been making many catches. To catch the game-winning touchdown is the thrill of a lifetime. It was huge.

We knew Kentucky would have time for one last drive. Sure enough, Couch started hitting his receivers again. They got deep in our end. I remember one play real well. Kenoy Kennedy hit their receiver so hard it knocked his helmet off and knocked him out. Man, Kenoy really hit that guy. We didn't know if he would get up.

After he left the field, Kentucky had time for another two plays. When both passes fell incomplete in the end zone, we celebrated. So did our fans. They stayed for what seemed like an hour after the game was over.

I remember what a great feeling it was after the game. It was great to beat Tim Couch and Kentucky. He was on all night. He found his receivers, but our defense never let down. They gritted their teeth and stopped Kentucky when we had to.

POSTGAME

Lucas had a sensational season in 1998. He bounced back quickly from the injury, and Arkansas won its first eight games. The Hogs thought they had made it nine in a row when they had top-ranked Tennessee down late in the game at Knoxville. However, a fumble allowed the Volunteers one last chance, and the Vols came back for a 28-24 win. Tennessee went on to win the national championship.

"It was a real special year," Lucas says. "We were one play away from playing for a national championship. We beat Tennessee up and down the field and everywhere but the scoreboard, and they beat Florida State in the national championship game.

"I loved the whole season. I was getting the ball, and the program had a great turnaround in Coach Nutt's first year. I love Coach Ford, but it was time for a change. Coach Nutt believed in the word *family* and that was a big part of our success."

In 1998 Lucas caught 43 passes and set school records with 1,004 receiving yards and 10 touchdowns. By the time his career concluded, he had 137 catches and established school standards for receiving yards with 2,879 and touchdowns with 23.

"I loved playing at Arkansas," Lucas says. "I hated to see it end. It was tough playing my last game. I'll never forget it. We beat Texas in the Cotton Bowl. Our fans were incredible. It was a great way to go out."

WHAT HAPPENED TO ANTHONY LUCAS?

Lucas graduated in 1999 and was drafted the following spring in the fourth round by Green Bay. He missed the 2000 season after having ACL surgery, and the Packers cut him in 2001.

Dallas quickly picked him up, but he broke a kneecap in October 2001 and again in August 2002. His football career had ended, and so he decided to return for more education.

"It was difficult giving up football," Lucas says. "My goal during my entire lifetime was to play pro football. Jerry Rice was my idol. To have it end was tough. I still miss it.

"But Coach Hill had earned a doctorate, and Marvin Caston got his master's, and that inspired me to go back to school."

Lucas finished work on his master's degree in the spring of 2005 while working. In June 2005, he became the executive director of LifeChamps, a youth sports organization in Little Rock.

CHAPTER 18

BARRY LUNNEY JR.

Born: September 11, 1974
Hometown: Fort Smith
Current Residence: Bentonville
Occupation: High School Assistant Football Coach
Position: Quarterback
Height: 6-2
Weight: 195
Years Lettered: 1992-1995
Accomplishments: Completed 476 of his 856 career passes for 5,782 yards and 33 touchdowns; was Arkansas's career passing leader when he graduated and still ranks second in total yards; passed for 2,181 yards in 1995 while leading the Razorbacks to their first ever Southeastern Conference Western Division title.
The Game: Arkansas vs. Tennessee, October 10, 1992, at Knoxville, Tennessee

BACKGROUND

B arry Lunney Jr. grew up around football. His father, Barry Sr., won four state championships as head coach at Fort Smith Southside High School before moving to Bentonville as head coach.

"Dad coached at Greenwood, Fordyce, and Beebe before we moved back to Fort Smith, where he had been an assistant once," Lunney says. "Being around him growing up acclimated me to football and eventually becoming a coach myself.

"At times it was difficult playing for my dad. In 1989 we only had five seniors at Southside, and I started at quarterback as a sophomore. We went 5-5, and some people criticized Dad for playing me. But after starting 1-2 in 1990, we won 22 of our next 24 games. We beat Little Rock Catholic when they were No. 1, reached the state semifinals my junior year, and won the state championship when I was a senior.

"I had always been around football. Dad was an assistant at Southside when I was nine years old. I rode the bus and was on the field for the state title game. Lou Holtz, who was the head coach at Arkansas then, did the color on the telecast. That was a hoot."

Recruiting was a pretty simple process for Lunney.

"My grandfather started for Arkansas in 1946 through 1949. He had season tickets, and I would go with him two or three times a year. We would always go through Apple Town. I thought the only way to get to Fayetteville from Fort Smith was Highway 59.

"Since my grandfather was a letterman, we would eat pregame brunch at the athletic dorm. Then we'd go to the Letterman's Club before sitting in the stands. I always took binoculars and watched the quarterbacks. I would watch everything they did from the pregame warmups on. I never dreamed I would someday be the Razorback quarterback. I thought of Arkansas as the best of the best. They were like a pro team to me."

Jack Crowe was Arkansas's head coach when Lunney was a senior in high school. But for Lunney it didn't really matter who was at the helm; the decision was made.

"I wasn't hard to recruit," Lunney admits. "Once I realized I had a chance to play at Arkansas, it was clear cut to me. Dad was more objective and thorough in his evaluation. He was concerned that Arkansas was running the option and not throwing a lot. That didn't matter to me.

"I committed before the playoffs. When they hired Greg Davis as offensive coordinator, I knew Arkansas would throw more. That sealed it for me. I had to fight not committing early in the year. If things had been like they are today, I would have been one of those players who committed during his junior year."

THE SEASON

J ason Allen was Arkansas's quarterback at the beginning of the 1992 season, Lunney's freshman campaign. Allen had quarterbacked the Hogs to a terrific start in 1991, their last year in the Southwest Conference, but hurt his knee against Baylor and underwent corrective surgery.

The Hogs joined the Southeastern Conference in August 1990, but the 1992 season was their first to compete in their new league. The season opener against The Citadel was supposed to be a warmup for the SEC season.

"I didn't play against The Citadel," Lunney says. "Coach Crowe had told me before the game I would play on the third series, no matter the circumstances. I could barely call the plays and formations. I was so nervous. The game started badly, and I wasn't sent into the game. I will never forget Coach Crowe turning and looking me right in the eye when that third series started. He didn't have to say a thing. I knew I wasn't going in. I was fine."

The Citadel shocked the Razorbacks 10-3. The defeat led to one of the most stunning moves in school history.

"I was watching NFL football on Sunday, and it came across the screen that Coach Crowe had been fired," Lunney says. "Nobody knew what was going on. Most of us didn't realize the implications of losing to someone like The Citadel. My freshman class was kicking off its career with instant instability.

"There we were in our first year in the SEC, and we went through instant growing pains. It was a mess. That loss had a major impact on the program. Our class was fighting an uphill battle from that point on."

Most of the Hogs thought Joe Pate, the assistant head coach, would be named temporary head coach but instead defensive coordinator Joe Kines received the position.

"I don't think there was a player on the team that didn't want Coach Kines as head coach. We trusted coach [Frank] Broyles to do the right thing, but we hoped we would play well enough for Coach Kines to get the job. At that time I didn't know much about coach [Danny] Ford's success at Clemson. I just liked Coach Kines."

Kines directed the Razorbacks to a runaway win at South Carolina in his first week as coach. The following week the Hogs entertained Alabama at Little Rock. The Crimson Tide would eventually win the national championship that year.

"I was strictly a backup quarterback at that point," Lunney says. "I had shadowed the coach during the Citadel and South Carolina games. I started that way against Alabama, but after I saw their defense I backed away. When I went into the game in the fourth quarter, I think their defense was tired from chasing Jason Allen.

"Actually Doyle Preston came in before me, but he fumbled the center exchange, and they put me in. That was my opportunity. I threw some swing passes, we moved the ball, and I threw a touchdown pass to Ron Dickerson on a slant pattern. Late in the game we almost scored again. Those drives gave me a little confidence."

Arkansas lost its next two games to Memphis State and Georgia. With a 1-3 record, the Razorbacks prepared to visit Tennessee at Knoxville.

THE SCENE

Tennessee was undefeated and was welcoming back head coach Johnny Majors, who had missed several games after surgery. The Volunteers were ranked fourth

Barry Lunney Jr.

nationally. More than 95,000 people filled their stadium every week. Arkansas was an overwhelming underdog.

"On Monday Coach Davis left a message for me to see him immediately," Lunney says. "I wondered what I had done. It never dawned on me I would start against Tennessee. When he told me I would start, I was excited. I called my dad right away. I talked to him frequently that week.

"All week Coach Kines played 'Rocky Top' on the loudspeaker to get us used to the noise. He must have played it a million times. That entire week was an experience I will never forget."

THE GAME
by Barry Lunney Jr.

I t was an early game since it was being televised by Jefferson-Pilot. When we went out for the warmups, there weren't very many people there. I was hoping the early kickoff would keep their crowd down. But when we came back out before kickoff, they were all there and they were right on top of us.

From the outset things went our way. I played as well as I possibly could. Jeff Savage had a good day running the ball, and the line blocked well. The first pass I hit was over the middle to Kirk Botkin. They almost sacked me on the play. It set up a field goal by Todd Wright, and that gave me some confidence.

I did throw an interception early that set up a touchdown for Tennessee. But that was my only interception of the day.

We got the lead back when I underthrew Ron Dickerson on a slant and go. He took it away from the defensive back and scored on a 50-yard play. I got smashed as I was throwing it. Still that gave me some confidence.

Late in the half I hit Ron again on a rollout for 20 yards. Todd boomed a field goal, and we had a 13-7 lead. It was quiet in that stadium.

After Todd kicked a 46-yard field goal in the third quarter, Tennessee got into the game. The crowd really got into it. We got stuffed on offense. I don't remember much of what happened other than Tennessee got tougher.

Late in the fourth quarter Tennessee had a 24-16 lead, but we made them punt. On the sidelines we were already thinking about a two-point play, because we knew we had to have eight points to tie. We assumed we would score. While we were thinking about what to call on the conversion attempt, Orlando Watters returned the punt 71 yards for a touchdown.

There were about two and a half minutes left when we scored. It helped we had talked about the two-point play, because we were prepared to run it. Someone missed an assignment, though, and I got sacked. It happened so fast. We only had one timeout left. When the attempt failed, the crowd exploded.

Then we tried an onside kick. Darwin Ireland recovered for us. I always admired Darwin a lot. He was a really good high school player. At Arkansas he was always around the ball. Once he got the onside kick, we knew we only needed a field goal, and Todd already had kicked three of them. At that point I thought we were supposed to win.

We started at the 50 but had a penalty and a sack and were facing third and 18. The line gave excellent protection, and I threw a desperation pass to Tracy Caldwell. He made a fantastic catch for a first down.

We were almost within field-goal range, and on third and three Coach Davis called a running play to get Todd a little closer. We still had that timeout. They jumped into a double eagle front, and I checked to a pass and hit Ron on the side-line for a first down. The coaches were surprised I changed the play, but I had been coached to do it in that situation.

We ran another play, called timeout, and left it to Todd. It would be a 41-yard attempt. I was talking to a Tennessee policeman on the sideline and didn't want to watch. Tennessee called two timeouts to try to freeze Todd, but Coach Kines kept smiling at him from the sidelines.

Finally Todd kicked it. From our angle we didn't know if it was good or not. I held my breath. When they signaled good, it was a great feeling. The kick came on the last play of the game, so Tennessee had no chance to come back.

My mom and many of my friends were there. Our team had been through a lot. The win was big for our program. It was embarrassing to lose to The Citadel, and Coach Crowe wasn't there. It was great for Coach Kines. It was a fun day and a very fun trip home.

POSTGAME

The rest of the 1992 season was a roller coaster for the Razorbacks. The week after upsetting Tennessee, the Hogs were beaten 17-3 by Ole Miss at Little Rock.

"I hated losing that game," Lunney says. "The week after beating Tennessee, everyone in the state was excited about coming back to Little Rock. I got a lot of credit for winning the game, but our defense was great, Watters made the big punt return, and Todd kicked the winning field goal.

"We were pretty beat up on the offensive line when we played Ole Miss, and we got flogged. Joe Lee Dunn was their defensive coordinator, and they pressured me all day. They sacked me nine times and hit me on every other play."

The Hogs finished 3-7-1 and hired Danny Ford as head coach. Lunney was the starting quarterback in 1993 and 1994 but always had to win his job back after pitching for UA baseball in the spring.

"Really, my career had been a disappointment through my first three years," Lunney says. "I envisioned more success. I was inconsistent during my sophomore year and had a pathetic game against Memphis when I missed open receivers. Then against Georgia I played as well as I could play. My junior year was inconsistent, too.

"At times I thought about leaving because I wasn't sure I fit the offense. During my sophomore and junior years, I was reading the triple option. When a quarterback runs 4.8 or 4.9 in the 40 and is reading the triple option, it really isn't your deal. But Coach Ford made us tougher, and I'm glad I stayed. I had hoped my last year would be a good one. I wanted to go out the right way.

Lunney was somewhat disappointed when Robert Reed started ahead of him at SMU, but he entered the contest on the third series and didn't allow not starting to bother him. He played the rest of the way.

"I was sharp that night," he recalls. "I ran well and made good decisions. Then we were going in for the winning touchdownwith about a minute left, and I fumbled the snap at the one. That fumble was devastating. I hit the wall."

Reed quit the team the next day, and Ford summoned his seniors for a meeting.

"I took the blame for the loss," Lunney says. "The seniors rallied around me. Earl Scott, Spencer Brown, Verl Mitchell, and Steven Conley stepped up on my behalf. There were others, too. That rallied us. And when Robert left, I was the quarterback.

Arkansas won eight of its next nine games and earned its first-ever SEC Western Division title. Lunney's last-second touchdown pass to J.J. Meadors gave the Hogs a one-point win at Alabama to spark the title run.

"Really, the Alabama win was more meaningful than Tennessee," Lunney says. "When we beat Tennessee my freshman year, I thought that would happen a lot over the next few years. But it didn't. Beating Alabama was huge. That led to a championship and better recruiting.

"Plus, Alabama's stadium has more aura than any in the SEC. Tennessee is overwhelming, and LSU is loud, but Alabama has the most tradition. That win got us over the hump of belonging in the SEC.

"As a senior class we felt like we laid the foundation for Arkansas in the SEC. We were the first Western Division team other than Alabama to play in the league championship game. The longer we're in the SEC, the more we realize how difficult it is to get to that championship game."

WHAT HAPPENED TO BARRY LUNNEY JR.?

After his senior year Lunney gave pro football a very brief try and then returned to pitch for the baseball Hogs. He signed with the Minnesota Twins and spent a year in the minor leagues before deciding it was time to begin his coaching career.

He served a year as a graduate assistant for Houston Nutt at Arkansas and then went to Tulsa as an assistant coach for Keith Burns for three years. He spent two years as an assistant for Fitz Hill at San Jose State before he and his wife, Janelle, returned to northwest Arkansas. He is an assistant coach for his dad at Bentonville High School.

CHAPTER 19

BILL McCLARD

Born: October 15, 1949
Hometown: Norman, Oklahoma
Current Residence: Rogers
Occupation: Commercial Agent for Lindsey and Associates, a real estate firm
Position: Kicker
Height: 6-1
Weight: 195
Years Lettered: 1969-1971
Accomplishments: Was the first in a series of All-America kickers at Arkansas, earning the honors in 1970 and again in 1971; set school records for extra points made and attempted and the records are still standing; made 125 career extra points on 133 attempts; set a record of 50 PATs in 1970, which is still the best ever by a Razorback; became the first collegiate kicker to make a 60-yard field goal; made 29 of his 46 career field goal attempts.
The Game: Arkansas vs. SMU, November 14, 1970, at Fayetteville, Arkansas

BACKGROUND

G rowing up in Norman, Bill McClard was influenced not so much by the tough tradition of Oklahoma football as he was by his hard-working father.

"Dad was a ceramic tile contractor," McClard says. "When I was young, he told me I might not work, but I would be standing real close to where work is happening.

"I started working for my dad when I was 13. I mixed concrete and brought it in for my dad. I started with three-gallon buckets. By the time I was a senior in high school, I was carrying six-gallon buckets. Those weigh between 90 and 100 pounds. I got strong carrying those buckets up a flight of stairs.

"My senior year I won the state championship in the shot put with a throw of 61-6. I had hernia surgery two days later. That would still rank as a pretty good throw today, and I did it while I had a hernia.

McClard grew up with weights at a time when they weren't as popular with athletes as they later became. When he was in the NFL he bench-pressed 425 pounds.

"I was one of the few guys I knew who used weights," McClard says. "I had my own set. I was an offensive lineman at 195 pounds. I needed to be strong."

McClard also was a kicker. He had kicked off for his sixth grade team when he was in the fifth grade. He started kicking early in life.

"In our backyard we had telephone poles that were great targets," McClard says. "I kicked over the tallest wires. When we played touch football, I would always kick the extra points.

"I was already good at kicking off as a ninth grader. I remember my ninth-grade coach telling me if I would give up kicking, I could be a pretty good offensive tackle. Fortunately, my high school coach had a different idea. He wanted me to kick as a sophomore. Back then sophomores didn't play much in high school. I was one of two sophomores who got to ride on the team bus."

During his high school career McClard tried four kicks of at least 50 yards. He made three of them. He kicked field goals of 53, 54, and 56 yards. At that time the NFL record for longest field goal was 56 yards. He kicked his 53-yarder at Owen Field because his high school team played in the stadium that housed Oklahoma football. It was longer than any field goal ever made by a Sooner kicker.

The recruiting process was different than it is today, but McClard had plenty of choices. He narrowed the decision to Oklahoma, Texas, and Arkansas.

"The OU coaches were there a lot naturally," McClard says. "It's hard to imagine growing up in Norman and considering Texas, but their tradition was neat and at that time they were beating OU nearly every year.

"Coach [Frank] Broyles was in my home eight times and Jim Lindsey, who had played at Arkansas and was with the Minnesota Vikings at the time, came to Norman every Thursday to take me to lunch. I found out later that Coach Broyles had told Jim to make sure I came to Arkansas.

"When we visited Fayetteville the sign on the Holiday Inn said, 'Welcome Bill McClard and family.' My parents were real impressed by that. Arkansas's facilities at the time were horrible. They didn't compare to OU's or Texas's. But Texas had a kicker, and Chuck Fairbanks, OU's coach, was honest enough to tell me they had signed a kicker, and I would probably redshirt after my freshman year. I thought I was better than that.

"Coach Broyles told me there would be a lot of opportunities for a kicker to score points with the team he was putting together. He was right. By the time I was through I had the NCAA records for points by a kicker and for extra points."

When McClard enrolled at Arkansas, freshmen weren't eligible to play for the varsity. He found kicking easy but school extremely difficult.

"I had dyslexia but didn't know it until long after I graduated," McClard says. "I started as an accounting major. I would know the answers but get them wrong on the tests. I thought I was stupid. God smiled on me, and I got a degree. I never missed a class. I studied and took the tests but barely got by.

"Football was the easy part. I felt comfortable kicking 53- and 54-yard field goals in practice, but until you do it in a game, you aren't validated. I only tried three field goals longer than 50 yards while at Arkansas and made them all. That means in high school and college I tried seven field goals longer than 50 yards and made six of them.

"I had a real strong leg. At the beginning of the 1969 season I was kicking field goals and extra points but wasn't kicking off. We would practice kicking the ball into the corner to make returns more difficult. One day I asked Merv Johnson, my assistant coach, why we didn't just kick it out of the end zone, eliminating any chance of a return.

"With Coach Broyles up in his tower and asking Merv what he was doing, he let me practice kickoffs. After I kicked five in a row out of the end zone, I had the job."

McClard knew he had all of the physical attributes of a great kicker, but he had to adjust to the mental side.

"In my first varsity game I missed two extra points against Oklahoma State," McClard recalls. "I only missed eight in my entire career, and two came in my first game. I got better as the year progressed."

McClard's first year was a great one for the Razorbacks. They won their first nine games to set up The Big Shootout with Texas in the regular-season finale at Fayetteville. The Longhorns were ranked first nationally, and the Hogs were No. 2. Midway through the fourth quarter Arkansas was nursing a 14-8 lead and had a third down inside the Texas 10. A field goal would have forced Texas to score twice to win. On third down, though, Arkansas suffered an interception in the end zone, and McClard never got the opportunity he had dreamed about. Texas won 15-14 on a late touchdown.

"I will always wonder if I would have made that kick against Texas," McClard says. "It wasn't much farther than an extra point. It would have put us in the Cotton Bowl, and it might have been Arkansas rather than Texas winning the national championship that year. I had worked all my life to get to that point and never got the opportunity. I'd had a good game the previous week against Texas Tech.

"I don't think about it much anymore during the normal course of my life, but there are still times when I am in Razorback Stadium when I think about it."

THE SEASON

After finishing 9-2 in 1969, Arkansas was one of the preseason national championship favorites in 1970. Once again the Texas game was moved to the final week of the campaign.

"I was in great shape," McClard says. "I lost 24 pounds on my summer job. I was really kicking well. We felt very good about our team. We were loaded with seniors. We knew we would be good."

As expected, the Razorbacks started strong. After a narrow first-game loss to Stanford, quarterbacked by eventual Heisman Trophy winner Jim Plunkett, Arkansas pounded Oklahoma State, Tulsa, TCU, Baylor, Wichita State, Texas A&M, and Rice. McClard rarely missed. He set a school record with a 53-yard field goal against Wichita State.

THE SCENE

SMU threw more than anyone in the Southwest Conference at the time McClard kicked for the Razorbacks. In 1969, Arkansas's 28-15 victory over the Mustangs at Dallas was its closest win of the year.

In 1970 SMU was not quite as good. The Razorbacks were expected to win and win big when the Mustangs came to Fayetteville. It was not the game but what happened that proved significant to McClard and the Hogs.

"It wasn't that big a game," McClard says. "Everyone assumed we would win by 20 to 25 points. The wind was blowing out of the north at 10 to 15 miles per hour. It was an ideal day for field goals. In the warmups I hit six out of eight tries from 68 yards away. I knew there would be an opportunity for something special."

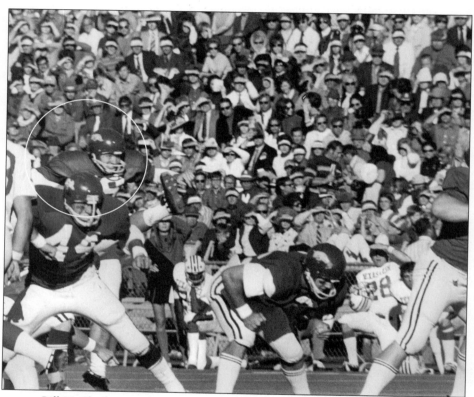

Bill McClard

THE GAME
by Bill McClard

Our defense gave SMU fits all day. We intercepted nine of their passes. That's still a school record. David Hogue had three interceptions himself. I kicked a couple of field goals, and Bill Montgomery had a touchdown run to give us the lead late in the second quarter.

It was just about halftime, and we had the wind at our back. We were in position to try a 60-yard field goal. Coach Broyles called for the punt team. I said to Merv Johnson, "Coach, let me try this. I can make it."

He asked Coach Broyles to let me kick.

The NCAA record at that point was 57 yards. I wanted to beat that. I knew I could kick it through, especially with the wind at my back.

Gus Rusher was the holder. He was really good, but for some reason on this kick, the ball came back, and he placed the laces toward me. Normally the holder will spin the laces away from the kicker, but I guess he didn't have time to do that. Normally you lose five or six yards when you kick the laces. For a kicker, the laces are a bad thing.

As a kicker you see all that, but you can't stop. You have 1.3 seconds from the snap to when the ball needs to be in the air.

I hit the ball solidly, but it was lower than it should have been for that distance. Laces. That was the reason. You just don't get the trajectory when you kick on the laces. But the wind helped, the ball hit the crossbar, and it went through.

I jumped sky high. I was shocked it went through since I kicked on the laces. I was so excited. The crowd went crazy. It was the first kick of that distance in NCAA history. You can kick 60-yarders every day in practice, but you aren't validated as a kicker until you do it in a game.

I was on cloud nine. They brought me the football at halftime. I got to keep the ball and still have it to this day.

In the second half I missed a field goal I should have made. We won the game easily, though, and breaking an NCAA record was a significant event in my life. It was like setting a world record.

POSTGAME

The next day was Bill McClard Day on campus.

"I had gone from being a good kicker to one that gained national attention," he says. "People knew my name. Even today people are likely to remember me as the kicker.

"That kick was the highlight of my career. I only kicked eight field goals that year because we scored so many touchdowns. After the Texas Tech game Coach Johnson told me I had made All-American. That was really something."

McClard was All-America in 1971, his senior season, as well. He thinks the best kick he had as a Razorback came that year.

"The 60-yarder was great because it had never been done, but I kicked a 47-yard field goal in our last regular-season game at Texas Tech that was better. It was against a real strong wind. I popped it as good as I've ever hit a kick. But it was *only* 47 yards. When you make one from 60, you are supposed to make those no matter how strong the wind is.

"It's the same as it is in life. Sometimes your best deal isn't the biggest."

WHAT HAPPENED TO BILL McCLARD?

McClard signed with the San Diego Chargers after completing his career at Arkansas. He kicked two field goals against Denver in the last game of his rookie season, but the Chargers didn't bring him back the following year.

He spent time in Atlanta before being picked up by New Orleans during the middle of the season.

"They called me during the week and said they needed a kicker, and I flew to meet the team. I didn't know a single player on the team, but that Sunday I was the kicker. I kicked four field goals in six tries, we beat Washington, and I was named Saint of the Week. I didn't even know the holder's name, but I was Saint of the Week."

One of his favorite NFL memories is the only conversation he ever had with pro football legend George Blanda.

"He was watching me kick and told me if we had his brain and my leg, we could kick forever," McClard recalls.

In his fourth season in the NFL McClard started having back problems. He missed three field goals in a game. All were attempts of 42 yards or longer, and all were against the wind.

"I hit them well but didn't make them," McClard says. "The next day John North, who was the head coach, told me one of us was getting fired, and I was going first."

During the offseasons McClard had been selling real estate in Little Rock and he turned to the profession full time. Several teams called trying to get him to sign, but he was doing better financially selling property than he had kicking footballs.

He spent 21 years in Little Rock before moving to northwest Arkansas to work for the same Jim Lindsey who had recruited him to Arkansas the first time. When he isn't on the job, he spends time with his wife, Paula; his son, Matthew, 27; his daughter, Rachel, 24; and his stepson, Ben, 22.

CHAPTER 20

J.J. MEADORS

Born: April 18, 1961
Hometown: Ruston, Louisiana
Current Residence: Dallas, Texas
Occupation: Pharmaceutical Sales for Pfizer
Position: Wide Receiver
Height: 5-6
Weight: 153
Years Lettered: 1992-1995
Accomplishments: Still holds the UA single-season reception record with 62 catches in 1995; made 134 career catches, a record at the time and currently fifth best ever at Arkansas; had 1,651 career yards and 10 touchdowns.
The Game: Arkansas vs. Alabama, September 16, 1995, at Tuscaloosa, Alabama

BACKGROUND

S ize was never a handicap to J.J. Meadors. His father was a wide receivers coach at Northwestern Louisiana, and Meadors grew up around the sport. He watched his father work with future NFL players Al Edwards, Odessa Turner, and Floyd Turner.

"I picked up routes at that time," Meadors says. "I was in the third or fourth grade when Dad started coaching at Northwestern Louisiana. We were there until my sophomore year in high school."

They moved to Ruston when Meadors was a sophomore. His dad sold insurance for a while before going back into coaching.

"I had a great high school career," Meadors recalls. "I was more noted for track than football. I was the state runner-up in the 100 and the 400 relay. There were some big-time schools recruiting me for track. My senior year more schools started recruiting me for football.

"I had a storybook year. Everything went well. I returned a couple of kickoffs and some punts for touchdowns. I had some long touchdown receptions and some long runs. When I played defense, I made some interceptions and even returned some of those for touchdowns. I had to do those kinds of things. At five foot six and 135 pounds, I didn't know if anyone would give me a shot."

Arkansas was more than interested in giving Meadors a shot. His uncle, Johnnie, was a starting defensive end on the Hogs' 1975 Southwest Conference championship team.

"I knew about the Razorbacks," Meadors says. "Johnnie was from Haynesville, a small town about 30 miles from Magnolia, Arkansas. I followed their football program. I knew about James Shibest, Steve Atwater, and Barry Foster."

Sam Goodwin, a former Razorback assistant who had become head coach at Northwestern Louisiana, recruited Meadors, but the Razorbacks also utilized defensive line coach Bill Johnson in the recruiting process.

"Coach Johnson and my dad coached together at Northwestern Louisiana," Meadors explains. "I had known him since the third grade. That gave Arkansas the inside track. I also considered Nebraska, but it was too far away. I wanted to play where my parents wouldn't have to go too far to see me. Plus, I met John McDonnell, the track coach, on my recruiting trip. Arkansas was a natural fit."

Meadors was a freshman at Arkansas in 1992. He was the only wide receiver the Hogs signed that year.

"The seniors made fun of me," Meadors recalls. "I was so short, they couldn't believe I was the only receiver in the entire freshman class."

His first month on campus was eventful to say the least. The Razorbacks lost to The Citadel in the season opener and head coach Jack Crowe was fired.

"This may sound strange, but I didn't know Coach Crowe that well," Meadors says. "Houston Nutt was my position coach, and we had built a good relationship. I was so new it didn't affect me that much. Then, after making just one catch, I dislocated my shoulder and missed the rest of the season."

Danny Ford was named head coach at the end of the 1992 campaign, and Meadors was encouraged to give up football or transfer.

"We needed players," Meadors says. "We were in the SEC. Coach Ford was looking at a five-foot-six receiver who had undergone reconstructive shoulder surgery. He told me if I wanted to run track full time, that would be okay. Rehabbing the shoulder injury I had was as tough as an ACL.

"I wasn't a quitter. I would rather stay than give up. Deep down I felt I could play at that level, and Arkansas is where I wanted to play."

Nutt left to become head coach at Murray State, and Fitz Hill joined the staff as a graduate assistant who would work with receivers.

"He had been a graduate assistant at Northwestern Louisiana and knew my dad," Meadors explains. "He encouraged me and worked with me. I had a great summer working with John Stucky in the weight room. I made the 'Men of Summer' poster that year.

"I went into the fall of 1993 as a second-team receiver behind Tracy Caldwell. Kotto Cotton was the other starting wideout. A stress fracture caused Tracy to miss the first two games of the year, and I got the opportunity to catch some balls. Tracy was a senior and the go-to receiver, but his injury gave me the chance to play."

Arkansas opened the season at SMU and trailed most of the way. A late march netted the touchdown that gave the Hogs a 10-6 triumph.

"I caught a pass that got us into scoring position on that last drive against SMU," Meadors says. "It's one thing to have potential. When you actually make a play, you realize you can play. It just takes a while to get used to the speed of the game. There's a world of difference between high school and the SEC."

Meadors's biggest highlight of his sophomore season was a 70-yard touchdown reception against Georgia.

"We got back to Fayetteville, and I called my dad," Meadors recalls. "While I was on the phone to him, both of us were watching *SportsCenter* on ESPN. As they went to a commercial, they showed my touchdown against Georgia. That's when college football started becoming fun."

Before his junior season Hill, by then the full-time receivers coach, challenged Meadors to be a leader and continue to make an impact.

"I remember making two touchdown catches against Vanderbilt that year," Meadors explains. "Anthony Eubanks caught a touchdown pass in that game, too. Later we beat Ole Miss. Those were our best games that year."

THE SEASON

Arkansas had finished 4-7 in 1994. In the spring of 1995 Ford brought the seniors together for a meeting that would change the direction of Razorback football.

"Coach Ford changed a little in 1995," Meadors says. "He wanted to know what we, the seniors, thought. The seniors took over the team. Coach Hill challenged me again. One evening he took me out for a hamburger and showed me one of the preseason magazines that had picked me second-team All-SEC. He told me people respected me but that brings expectations. I was excited."

Two weeks before the season opener at SMU, Meadors injured a knee in a blocking drill. He made it back for the first game, but the Hogs suffered a stunning upset defeat. Trailing 17-14, Arkansas marched to the SMU one with less than a minute left, but a fumbled snap was recovered by the Mustangs.

"We were disappointed to say the least, but looking back, it was the best thing that happened to us," Meadors says. "The seniors met together the next morning and later that day with Coach Ford. Barry Lunney, our quarterback, was really down about fumbling the snap. He tried to apologize, but before he could, the rest of the guys stopped him.

"Guys like Spencer Brown, Earl Scott, Mike Nunnerley, and Steve Conley reminded all of us that we had 10 games left. SMU wasn't a conference game. We had plenty of time left. We got on a roll from there."

The Razorbacks blasted South Carolina in their second game, with Madre Hill scoring six touchdowns. It set up an early-season showdown at Alabama.

THE SCENE

Alabama has always been a big game for the Razorbacks, and the 1995 matchup was no different. Going into the game, the team was more than aware of the history and the significance of this meeting.

"In 1992, my first year at Arkansas and our first season in the SEC, Alabama was a power," Meadors says. "We saw some great teams during my career at Arkansas, but that 1992 Alabama team was the best. They had 10 or 12 players that not only made it to the NFL, they were good.

"The 1995 season was the first time I really felt we had a chance to win the game. We were well prepared, and we were clicking. Besides Madre, Barry had really played well against South Carolina.

"At our Friday walkaround at the stadium, I thought about the 1993 game when Alabama beat us 43-3 and Antonio Langham returned an interception for a touchdown. That year Joe Kines, our defensive coordinator, told us that we worked all week to put money in the bank, but on Saturdays we didn't write big enough checks."

J.J. Meadors

Meadors, Lunney, Junor Soli, and Tracy Cantlope were the captains that day.

"The stadium was packed," Meadors remembers. "We knew it would be a tough game. Alabama is always tough on defense.

"During the pregame warmups coach [Joe] Pate came up to me and told me that Brother Oliver, Alabama's defensive coordinator, had told him I was one of the most dangerous players in the SEC. Coach Pate told me I should be able to score from anywhere on the field. That was a nice compliment."

THE GAME
by J.J. Meadors

I really had a bad day until the fourth quarter. Madre Hill had a great first quarter, and we were ahead 10-3. Then Alabama came back to take a 17-10 halftime lead. We had a senior-laden team, so we didn't panic when we were behind. We knew we were good and that we wouldn't beat ourselves. A seven-point deficit was nothing to worry about.

In the second half it rained at times, and I misplayed a punt. We hadn't thrown much, and when you go 15 to 20 plays without touching the ball, it's hard to stay focused. The punt was a short one, and I took my eye off it for a second. I let it hit, and Alabama downed it at the one. On the next play they tackled Madre for a safety to make it 19-10.

When you are five foot six and 150 pounds, if you aren't confident, you can't play with guys like Alabama had. You have to be mentally strong, because you aren't going to intimidate anyone. After letting that punt hit, I lost my edge.

We were still down by nine when Mark Smith made a huge interception and returned deep into Alabama territory. We kicked a field goal to pull within six.

Our defense was remarkable the entire second half. Alabama only made one first down in the entire half. The defense really kept us in the game.

In the fourth quarter we had a chance to kick another field goal, but the rain and wind came up and we messed up the snap. After that the sun came back out again.

We got the ball back at our 43 with a little over three minutes left. The first play we called was a post route. I beat the defensive back, and it should have been a touchdown. I was running full speed and lunged for the ball. I misplayed it and missed it.

When I came back to the huddle, I was thinking that this was my fourth year in college, and I was still making mistakes. Barry told me not to worry about it and that we would get it back later. Then he got sacked, and we were facing fourth and 16.

On the next play Barry was about to get sacked when he saw Anthony Lucas and hit him for a 31-yard gain. That was the first big catch of Anthony's career. It kept us going.

After that, we called a smash route and I was the outside receiver. I ran a hitch, and the inside receiver ran a flag route. They were in man defense, I ran a shallow crossing route, and the defensive back went for the interception. He missed it, and it went into my hands. It got to the three.

At that point we were tired. We were in the two-minute offense, and I didn't go back to the huddle. I would look at the sidelines for the play, and I would tell Anthony Eubanks what it was. We called timeout, and Coach Hill asked what we were doing. He made us go back to the huddle.

On third down we brought Cory Nichols into the backfield because he was a little better receiver than Madre. The only problem was Madre didn't leave the game. We had 12 men on the field. The play only gained a yard, but the officials missed the penalty. If they had called it, we would have had fourth down at the 18 instead of the three.

Gene Stallings, the Alabama coach, saw it. He was upset. That officiating crew was suspended by the SEC for the next week.

On fourth down we lined up with Eubanks in the slot, and I was the flanker. I went in motion. The ball was supposed to go to me, and my job was to get open. I slid inside Eubanks, and his man slid over and took me. I opened up and ran away from him. I was wide open, but Barry flipped it toward the ground.

In practice we had a bad ball drill where Coach Hill would throw it too high and too low to us. He always taught us to get our hands in the proper position, and if the ball was low to go to our knees.

So I went to my knees. The ball was real low. I got my hands down on the ground and caught it. I jumped up and saw the official signal touchdown. I didn't realize how close it was until I got back to Fayetteville and saw it on television.

We were very excited after the game. It was the first time we had beaten Alabama. On the bus to the airport, the driver had a postgame call-in show on and the Alabama fans were saying I didn't catch the ball. I thought they were crazy.

When I got back to my dorm room, I had about 20 messages on my answering machine with friends asking if I really caught it. When I saw it on TV, I could understand why some people thought I didn't catch it. I can tell you this, though. That ball didn't hit the ground before I got my hands under it.

POSTGAME

Meadors caught a school-record 62 passes in 1995 as the Razorbacks won their first SEC Western Division title. He set a UA record, since broken, for career receptions with 134.

"It was really a fun year," Meadors says. "It wasn't our most talented team. My sophomore year we had players like Isaac Davis, Henry Ford, Orlando Watters, Darwin Ireland, Carl Kidd, and Tyrone Chatman. That was our most talented team.

"But we won, and we enjoyed each other. Our team was close. Earl Scott is my best friend to this day. I could name all the seniors in that group. We are friends for life. As a group we struggled a lot. We had some tough, tough times. We had to work extremely hard to enjoy the success we had in 1995."

WHAT HAPPENED TO J.J. MEADORS?

Meadors completed his degree work in December 1996 and worked for two years in Shreveport for Wal-Mart. He then moved to Dallas, working two years for Xerox before joining Pfizer in his current position.

CHAPTER 21

JAMES ROUSE

Born: December 18, 1966
Hometown: Little Rock
Current Residence: Little Rock
Current Occupation: Financial Analyst for Stephens, Inc.
Position: Halfback
Height: 6-1
Weight: 215
Years Lettered: 1985, 1987-1989
Accomplishments: Rushed for 2,887 yards during his career, fourth best ever by a Razorback; gained 1,004 yards in 1987 becoming just the third Hog to earn at least 1,000 yards in a season; ran for 38 touchdowns, second highest total ever at Arkansas; got 219 yards against New Mexico, the fourth highest single-game total in UA history.
The Game: Arkansas vs. New Mexico, November 28, 1987, at Little Rock, Arkansas

BACKGROUND

J ames Rouse cried the first year he played football. He was only six, and his
father started him in a recreational league with seven-, eight- and nine-year-
olds.

"I'd get hit and cry," Rouse says. "I had wanted to play football, and my
dad said I was getting what I had asked for. He told me it was a tough game.
Actually, I did pretty well. I was a running back from the first day I played football.

"The next year I played in a city league with players my age. I ran crazy. It
was the start of a good career for me. My dad told me I would be good. He built
toughness into me.

"In our neighborhood I became a household name. Everyone knew I was
gonna be good. I didn't think about it. I was just having fun. I wasn't that big. I
went from 165 pounds my ninth grade year to 185 as a sophomore. I sprouted
out but kept my speed. I ran track, too. In fact, I was running the 100- and 200-
meter dashes in national meets when I was 11 and 12. I knew I was fast when I
finished second in the 100 and third in the 200."

At Little Rock Parkview he started his third game as a sophomore.

"It never registered how good I was compared to others," Rouse confesses.
"I didn't know. We tied for the conference title my sophomore year, and we were
13-0 into the state championship game my junior season. I only played one full
game my junior year because we were usually way ahead by halftime.

"Keith Jackson, Rickey Williams, and Anthony Chambers were on that
team. Scouts were there all the time watching us.

"I committed to Arkansas early in my senior season. My dad stepped in.
He didn't want me to go through the recruiting process. When I committed, it
put pressure on the other good players in the state—Freddie Childress, Elbert
Crawford, Anthony Cooney, and the others—to commit early.

"Looking back, I wish I would have made some trips. The only place I went
besides Arkansas was Oklahoma. I went to OU because Keith Jackson was there.
But I knew I wanted to be a Hog. Recruiting can be a headache if you drag it out."

Rouse was one of the most highly rated backs in Arkansas in years, but he
knew it wouldn't be easy in college.

"My coach told me it was a different ballgame," he explains. "There is a lot
more competition. Arkansas signed Joe Johnson out of Texas, and he was very
highly regarded. I didn't know if I would redshirt as a freshman. I was determined to do the best I could, and whatever happened would happen."

Under coach Ken Hatfield the Razorbacks were running the Wishbone
offense when Rouse reported in the fall of 1985.

"I had to make a lot of adjustments," Rouse says. "We had run the I offense
in high school. I had good peripheral vision, and in the I, a back can see where
to go when the hole opens.

"In a three-point stance out of the Wishbone, you can't see the field. When the defense switches, you can't see it. You have to adjust on the run. In the I, you can adjust before you get to the line of scrimmage. It took a while for me to adjust to the three-point stance and to block. I did very little blocking in high school. In the Wishbone you always block when you don't have the ball."

He set a school record for most rushing yards by a freshman in 1985 and says his coming-out game was against Texas.

"We lost 15-13 when they kicked five field goals, but I had a good game," Rouse admits. "That's when I learned I could play on the major college level. We were ranked high before the game. If we had won that game, I really believe we could have won the national championship."

Expectations were high for Rouse in 1986, but early in the season he suffered a broken leg and was shelved for the season. He received a medical hardship and was back in time for spring practice in 1987.

THE SEASON

Rouse knew the Razorbacks would be good in 1987.

"We had all the key ingredients in the right places," he says. "But games are won on the field, not on the sidelines. I thought I would have a good year. I had never missed any time with an injury before 1986. In high school I played with an ankle sprain, a bruised thigh, and a bruised knee. I never missed a game.

"It's a lonely feeling when you are hurt. You feel forgotten even when you know you are a good player. They have to go on without you if you can't contribute. It took me a while to get into the right mental frame to play again. You always wonder if it's going to pop again. That's over after the first couple of hits."

Arkansas was ranked in the top 10 and was 2-0 when Miami came to Little Rock. Hog hopes were high, but they were quickly shattered.

"On our first drive I thought we could play with Miami," Rouse says. "We missed a field goal, and the route started. We got so far behind so fast that we tried to throw for most of the game, and I didn't carry the ball much."

The Razorbacks rebounded to beat TCU and Texas Tech but lost on the last play of the game to Texas in Little Rock. It was a devastating defeat that put pressure on Hatfield and the entire team.

"We were down after losing to Texas," Rouse remembers. "We wondered how we could have let that happen. We questioned ourselves. We were all upset. But we had to move on. We figured anyone could lose, and if we took them one at a time, we could still win the conference."

Victories over Houston, Rice, and Baylor kept the Hogs in the race, but a loss at Texas A&M eliminated them from a shot at the SWC title. Most Razorback fans were disappointed with the 7-3 record the Hogs took to Little Rock for a non-conference game with New Mexico.

James Rouse

THE SCENE

An Arkansas grad and one of the heroes of the 1964 national championship team, Hatfield had led the Razorbacks to 19 wins in the previous two seasons, but the losses to Miami and Texas in 1987 put him under some fire.

"We weren't that aware of it," Rouse says. "I never read the newspapers. We knew there was some negative talk, but Coach Hatfield didn't want us caught up in it. We tried to just play."

The Hogs had two weeks to recover from the loss at Texas A&M, but they weren't at their emotional best for the New Mexico game. The Razorbacks figured to win easily, and perhaps the unrest over Hatfield would disappear.

Rouse had other problems. He was sick the night before the game.

"I felt better in the morning, but I wasn't doing very well before the game," he confesses. "They gave me something for my stomach, but I was nauseous."

THE GAME
by James Rouse

I started the game even though I felt terrible. Early in the game I had a 42-yard run for a touchdown, and we built a comfortable 16-0 lead. I was having a hard time, though. I kept coming to the sidelines and throwing up.

Near the end of the first quarter, I started getting chills. I threw up into a big garbage can, and I knew I was low on fluids. I told Dean Weber, our trainer, I just couldn't go any farther. They took me into the dressing room.

I wasn't planning on playing anymore. I was in the dressing room with my pads off and laying on a table. They had given me some medicine. All of the sudden I heard the door slam and in came my dad.

He told me the team needed me. Arkansas was losing. I thought he was kidding. I was out of it. He told me I'd be okay. I didn't want to go back at all, but my dad told me to put my clothes on and get back out there.

I came back just after the third quarter started. Sure enough, New Mexico was ahead 17-16. They had a great receiver named Terrance Mathis. We couldn't stop him. He made 14 catches and had over 200 yards receiving. He had a great, great day.

If we hadn't been behind, I wouldn't have gone back into the game. I knew I would have to gut it out and do whatever I could do to make things happen. I knew if I got hit, I could throw up again.

We really had a great offense when we were healthy. Greg Thomas and Quinn Grovey, our quarterbacks, had been injured most of the year. Both of them were talented. Quinn is a great guy. We gave him a hard time because a lot of times he wouldn't pitch it to us. We had a song titled "Quinn, Please Pitch Us The Ball." But Quinn added so much to our offense. His shiftiness made defenders look silly.

Greg had a better arm and could throw better than Quinn. He was more precise. But Quinn could change a game in a second. Even with both of them hurt, we knew we could come back against New Mexico.

Once I went back in, I had one of the best games of my career. I scored the next three touchdowns and we were back in control. I didn't have that many carries (19), but I ran for 219 yards and had a 70-yard run called back.

We won the game by 18 points. I showered, and then they took me to the doctor. I had a productive game, but it wasn't a fun time. It's hard to throw up and come back to play.

POSTGAME

Victories over New Mexico and Hawaii probably saved Hatfield's job. After the game, most of Rouse's teammates gave him credit for the victory. Hatfield admitted Rouse's return was the difference in the game. Had Rouse not come back out to play, there is no guarantee Arkansas would have won.

"We didn't know what was going on with the coaches," Rouse says. "We heard stories, but didn't think they would fire Coach Hatfield. It was all about winning big games, not just being 8-3. Looking back, if we had lost to New Mexico, Coach Hatfield could have been fired. It happened to Jack Crowe after losing to The Citadel."

Rouse wasn't as close to Hatfield as he was to running backs coach Larry Brinson.

"I wasn't much of a talker," Rouse explains. "Coach Hatfield would push you to get better and then give you a pat on the back. I only saw him at team meetings and on the field."

Hatfield and the Hogs recovered nicely. Given a reprieve, Hatfield led the Razorbacks to back-to-back SWC championships and a pair of trips to the Cotton Bowl.

"I didn't play that much in 1988," Rouse says. "I was hurt again. I only played one down against UCLA in the Cotton Bowl.

"My best memories as a Razorback came in 1989. We had an exceptional year. We hit on all cylinders and made it back to the Cotton Bowl. That was big for me since I played so little the previous year.

"Our last game in Little Rock was emotional for me. A bunch of little kids in jerseys with my number on them came down on the field to get their pictures made with me. That was quite a moment.

"At the Cotton Bowl, I had a great first half against Tennessee. I rushed for 117 yards in that first half. Our ground game was going, but we turned the ball over three times deep in Tennessee territory.

"I was never one to question our coaches, but we got away from our game plan in the second half. It's easy to have hindsight, but at the time I wondered why we didn't keep running the ball. Later when I was with the Bears one of my teammates was Anthony Morgan who played at Tennessee. He admitted they couldn't stop me or our running game. He said he remembered I was killing them."

WHAT HAPPENED TO JAMES ROUSE?

Drafted by the Bears, Rouse enjoyed his time in the NFL.
"It was a great experience," he explains. "I knew I could play in the NFL. The Bears had Neal Anderson, and he was their top ball carrier. They moved me to fullback. I'd never played without the ball in my hands.

"I played quite a bit as the backup my first year, and then I started five or six games in my second season. I was picking up the position well. They gave me the ball some and threw it to me, too. I made eight or nine catches in a game against Tampa Bay. As a rookie I played on special teams and was second among special team players in tackles.

"Pro football was hard. Everyone was trying to get a job. Nothing was handed to you. You have to give your best every day or you can be gone quickly."

Rouse signed with the Bears for his third season and had a great preseason.

"All of a sudden, though, we went to a one back set, and they were only going to keep one fullback," Rouse remembers. "I got cut late, and by then everyone's rosters were set. I almost signed with the Jets, but it didn't work out.

"I was going to play for Atlanta in 1993 and had an okay preseason before I hurt my shoulder. By the time I was healthy, it was too late to make the team. I gave up after that. I knew I could play but didn't have an opportunity. My football career was done."

Rouse was living in Chicago at the time. He moved back to Little Rock and interviewed for a position with Stephens, Inc. He was hired and has worked there for 11 years. He currently serves as a financial analyst. He and his wife, Gina, have two children, James III "Trey," six, and Alexandria, two.

"I've known guys who never recover once their football career is over," Rouse says. "I craved football but realized at some point you have to let it go. It took me two or three years to get it out of my system. I can watch it on TV now, but for a long time I couldn't."

Nearly every day Rouse is reminded of his career as a Razorback.

"It's hard to go anywhere in Arkansas without being recognized," Rouse explains. "If you produce on and off the field, people respect you. The relationships you form with your teammates are second to none. We're still friends today and always will be."

CHAPTER 22

KEVIN SCANLON

Born: May 28, 1957
Current Residence: Little Rock
Occupation: Managing Director and Senior Vice President, Stephens Inc.
Position: Quarterback
Playing Height: 6-0
Playing Weight: 185
Years Lettered: 1978-1979
Accomplishments: Was Southwest Conference Player of the Year in 1979 when he set a school record that still stands by completing 66.2 percent of his passes (92 of 139); was All-SWC and honorable mention All-American; led the Razorbacks to a 10-1 regular season, a share of the SWC title, and a spot opposite top-ranked Alabama in the Sugar Bowl.
The Game: Arkansas vs. Texas, October 20, 1979, at Little Rock, Arkansas

BACKGROUND

As a senior at Beaver Falls (Pennsylvania) High School—the same school that produced Joe Namath, Kevin Scanlon received plenty of scholarship offers. He narrowed his choices to Notre Dame, Syracuse, and North Carolina State, then coached by Lou Holtz.

Ara Parseghian was the Notre Dame head coach who was recruiting Scanlon, but he retired following the 1974 season and was replaced by Dan Devine. Scanlon had been leaning toward Notre Dame, but Devine wanted film and was changing the offense.

"My high school coach told me that wasn't a good sign," Scanlon says. As Scanlon was beginning to doubt Notre Dame, Coach Holtz made a visit to his high school, mostly to look at a wide receiver.

"My high school coach was from East Liverpool, Ohio, the same hometown as Coach Holtz," Scanlon recalls. "Coach Holtz was watching film when I arrived. He told me to come back in an hour. When I returned, he told me he liked the wide receiver but wasn't going to offer him a scholarship.

"He turned some film on and started asking me questions. When we finished, he offered me a scholarship and set up a recruiting visit. I visited Syracuse first. It was cold and snowy. When I visited North Carolina State, it was much nicer and I really liked Coach Holtz. I met his family and the quarterbacks coach on my visit, and it seemed like the right place to go.

"When I told my dad I was ready to commit, I called North Carolina State. I talked to an assistant coach who didn't seem to know me. When I told him I wanted to commit, he told me he would call me back. I panicked a little. I thought they didn't want me anymore.

"My dad told me not to make any rash decisions. Shortly after that Coach Holtz called and was very excited. I confirmed my commitment and signed with NC State."

Scanlon's first year at NC State was even better than expected. He was the backup to senior Dave Buckey.

"I dressed and traveled to all the games," Scanlon says. "I held for extra points and field goals. We were getting beat bad against Michigan State so I got to play and led our team to two touchdowns.

"After my freshman season Coach Holtz left for the New York Jets and NC State hired Bo Rein. He changed the offense from the veer to a dropback attack and moved Johnny Evans from fullback to quarterback, where he had played the year before I got there. He told me to get bigger and stronger, but I broke my collarbone in the spring and entered the 1976 season as a backup."

Scanlon was a thrower while Evans was a runner. Evans started all season, and Scanlon had a miserable year.

"After the season I met with Coach Rein and told him I wanted to transfer," Scanlon says. "He talked me out of it, and I came back to have a good spring. I thought I would be the starter, but he told us after the spring that Evans would be No. 1 and I would be 1A. I decided to transfer.

"Arkansas, Pittsburgh, Tennessee, and UCLA were interested, but my first visit was to Arkansas. Coach Holtz had left the Jets to become head coach at Arkansas. He was nice to me when I visited. Pete Cordelli, an assistant coach, told me Coach Holtz probably would offer me a scholarship and that I should take it. I spent some time with Don Breaux, the quarterbacks coach. He offered me a scholarship, and I said yes. He told me about Ron Calcagni, Houston Nutt, and Mike Scott, but told me I would have an opportunity after sitting out a year.

"The year I redshirted Ron Calcagni had a fantastic year. The Razorbacks were 11-1 and beat Oklahoma in the Orange Bowl. I had two surgeries during the year after twice tearing ligaments in my left thumb. All I could do was throw, so every day in practice I threw against the No. 1 secondary. It was a great secondary, and it made me better. During the game I charted plays on the sidelines.

"Since Ron had played so well in 1977, Coach Holtz told me going into the 1978 season that I would be the backup, but that if I would do what I was supposed to do, I would help us win three games. I did the best I could and helped some. Being with Ron made me a better player.

"It was friendly competition. I needed that to improve. I hadn't played a lot, and I had transferred to a program at a higher level. I had to step up. I got stronger and become more aware of what was expected of a quarterback."

THE SEASON

Heading into the 1979 season Scanlon figured to be the clear-cut starter with redshirt freshman Tom Jones as No. 2. However, in the final preseason scrimmage Scanlon fumbled twice, and Holtz told him he wasn't sure about who would start.

"Coach Holtz told me I would start the season at quarterback, but I couldn't turn the ball over," Scanlon says. "He told me I wouldn't make All-Conference. He told me if I would just help the team win, I would have a great life because the people of Arkansas would always remember me. I asked him if he was trying to give me a pep talk. He said no, he was giving me a warning.

"As time went on, Coach Holtz gained confidence in me. We had a solid group of 13 seniors and a terrific freshman class. I learned pretty quickly how good the freshmen were. In our first scrimmage Gary Anderson returned a punt 70 yards for a touchdown. Then he broke a long run against the first defense. Coach Breaux told me to get to know Gary because he would be spending a lot of time in the huddle.

"Also, you could tell how special Billy Ray Smith would be on defense. There were a lot of good young players.

Kevin Scanlon

"We weren't expected to be very good. We had lost an exceptional senior class and were relying on a lot of new players. During two-a-days we could tell we would be much better than people thought."

Arkansas started 5-0 with victories over Colorado State, Oklahoma State, Tulsa, TCU, and Texas Tech. The only close call came against TCU where the Hogs needed a last-second field goal to win 16-13.

"Winning at the end of the TCU game was huge for our confidence," Scanlon says. "We made up a play and hit the tight end, Darryl Mason, deep for a long gain to set up the winning field goal. After we beat Texas Tech we were more than ready to play Texas."

THE SCENE

Arkansas had not defeated Texas since 1971 when Joe Ferguson passed the Longhorns silly in the rain at Little Rock. The Longhorns were ranked second nationally and were undefeated as they frequently were when playing the Razorbacks. The Hogs had moved to No. 10 nationally.

In 1977, Holtz's first year at Arkansas, Texas trimmed the Razorbacks 13-9. It was the only loss of the year for the Hogs and conceivably cost Arkansas a national title. In 1978 Texas handed Arkansas a 28-21 setback at Austin, one of just two losses all year for the Razorbacks.

"We knew they were good, but we were very calm about playing Texas," Scanlon says. "We thought we could compete with them. As always there was great anticipation on campus. When Arkansas plays Texas it's all anyone wants to talk about."

THE GAME
by Kevin Scanlon

War Memorial Stadium was packed. Our fans were starved to beat Texas. The entire state was pumped. We were pumped. We wanted to get off to a good start, but that didn't happen.

I threw a bomb on the first play of the game, and Texas intercepted it. That wasn't the only thing that went wrong. I was sacked three times in the first quarter. I had a hip pointer and came out for a series. This is the game I had dreamed about, and I didn't know if I would return.

Coach put Tom Jones in the game. On his first play he threw a beautiful long pass that should have been an 80-yard touchdown, but Bobby Duckworth dropped the ball. I thought that was it for me. But on second down, Jones got sacked. On third down they smashed him in the mouth. On the sidelines I thought it was unfair for a redshirt freshman to go through that.

Then Kevin Evans came up with an interception for us, and I told Coach Holtz I was ready to go back in. As it turned out I played the rest of the game.

It wasn't easy moving the ball against Texas. We finally got a good drive going in the second quarter. On third and 11 Coach Holtz called timeout and told me to run a middle screen to the tight end. I told him we didn't have it in our playbook. He said we had it at North Carolina State. He said to tell them how to run it and it would work.

We ran the play to Darryl Mason, and he made 10 3/4 yards. We didn't need much for the first down. On the next play we ran the option with Gary Anderson. From watching film we knew Gary could make a big play if we could get him one on one on the corner. Robert Farrell threw a great block on Johnny Johnson, their great safety. We didn't block the corner. Gary beat the guy and ran 28 yards for a touchdown. The play worked just like we had practiced it.

That tied the game, and that's the way it stayed until our defense forced a turnover in the third quarter. We needed a break and got one, but the first downs weren't coming easy.

On third and eight Mason told me, "Throw the ball to me."

I did for a first down. When we reached the Texas nine-yard line, I called Mason's number again.

We thought Darryl could run a crossing pattern and be open. Texas blitzed, I threw to Darryl in the corner of the end zone, and he made a great catch and we were ahead 14-7.

Later we went on one of our best drives of the season. We wanted to use the clock, and we grounded it out 70 yards in 18 plays. You could sense the confidence we were gaining. That drive bonded us for the rest of the year. On third and seven I ran the option for a first down. We had a second and 20 and ran a play we had never used. I threw a deep pass to Roland Sales, and it picked up 27 yards. Eventually Ish Ordonez kicked a field goal to give us a 17-7 lead with six minutes left.

Throughout history it has never been easy for Arkansas to beat Texas. We were all feeling good until they scored a fluke touchdown when a pass bounced out of a defender's hands into a receiver's in the end zone.

Late in the game Texas could have tied the game with a long field goal, but by that time we were so confident that we were determined to score if the field goal had been good. We were discussing what we would do on a final drive if necessary. We would not accept anything but a victory that day.

After the missed field goal, all we had to do was fall on the ball to kill the clock. The crowd was getting louder and louder with each expiring second. It was one of the highlights of my life. During the week the linemen had made me promise I would sing "Turn Out the Lights, the Party is Over," when I came to the line of scrimmage if we were running out the clock. I didn't want to do it, but a promise is a promise. It was so loud in the stadium I doubt anyone heard me.

People were so loud we could hardly hear ourselves. Thirty minutes after the game the fans were all still there. I had never experienced anything like it.

POSTGAME

S canlon, who had completed 65 percent of his passes in high school, hit 66.2 percent of his tosses in 1979 and led the Hogs to a share of the SWC title with Texas and Houston.

"We really became a team during that Texas game," Scanlon recalls. "After that we didn't think there was any situation we couldn't overcome. Baylor was ahead of us 17-0 in the third quarter of our homecoming game, but we caught up before Robert Farrell got behind their defense for the touchdown catch that won the game.

"My fondest and saddest moment was hearing our fans call the Hogs at the SMU game. I realized it was my last game in the state of Arkansas. I loved everything about my experience at Arkansas. It was extremely special.

"I earned a lot of honors that year, but they've been long forgotten. People haven't forgotten the Texas game, though. I get reminded about that game by someone just about every day.

"The 13 members of our senior class are still very close. Their phone numbers are all in my Rolodex. They are close friends. We have a special bond. I am still grateful for every day I had the opportunity to be the Razorback quarterback. There is a lot of pressure and a lot of responsibility in being the quarterback at Arkansas. But once you've done it, you will always be a Razorback.

"It even carries a sense of responsibility with it the rest of your life. It is a special status. People remember you. I still do some speaking all over the state, just because I played quarterback at Arkansas."

WHAT HAPPENED TO KEVIN SCANLON?

S canlon earned his bachelor's degree from Arkansas in December 1979. He interned on Governor Bill Clinton's staff in the summer of 1979, then worked on Clinton's staff for six months after he graduated.

He signed with the Los Angeles Rams but was released in training camp. After a brief time with Hamilton in the Canadian Football League, he worked for an advertising agency in Little Rock for 15 months. He was offered an opportunity to sign as a free agent with the Washington Redskins, but when his wife was pregnant with their second child, he decided to give up football.

Scanlon worked for Merrill Lynch for six and a half years before joining Stephens, Inc., in 1987. He's been there ever since.

He met his wife, Vicki, at North Carolina State. His son, Bryan, played baseball at Centenary and now works at Stephens, Inc. His oldest daughter, Leigh, has a master's degree from Arkansas and teaches at Forrest Park Elementary School. His other daughter, Laura, just graduated from Mt. St. Mary's.

CHAPTER 23

CLINT STOERNER

Born: December 29, 1977

Hometown: Baytown, Texas

Current Residences: Johnson, Arkansas, and Dallas, Texas

Occupation: Owner of Gutter Helmet of Northwest Arkansas; Arena League quarterback

Position: Quarterback

Height: 6-2

Weight: 220

Years Lettered: 1996-1999

Accomplishments: Was second-team All-Southeastern Conference in 1998 and 1999 while leading Razorbacks to 17 wins and two top 20 finishes; set UA records for passing yards in a game (387 vs. LSU), season (2,629 in 1998) and career (7,422); also set school career standards for touchdown passes (57) and total offense (7,049 yards, since broken).

The Game: Arkansas vs. Tennessee, November 13, 1999, Fayetteville, Arkansas

BACKGROUND

Clint Stoerner almost quit football long before he was a record-breaking quarterback at Arkansas. Baytown Lee High School in Texas turned out some of the best quarterbacks in the country during and after Stoerner's time there. Before his junior season his coach, Dick Olin, told him he would be the backup quarterback and a wide receiver that year.

"I wanted to be a quarterback," Stoerner says. "I was a pretty good baseball player, so I considered just playing one sport and quitting football. Coach Olin told me if I would stick with him, he would get me a division one scholarship. He was only in his second year at our school, so I don't know why I believed him but I did. As it turns out, his quarterbacks went to Baylor, Iowa, Utah, and Kansas State as well as me going to Arkansas."

So Stoerner wasn't a quarterback until his senior year. He still played baseball and can remember times in the spring when college scouts would be in town and he would throw a football while wearing his baseball uniform.

"There were about 10 schools interested in me," Stoerner says. "Oklahoma, Kansas State, LSU, and Arkansas are the ones I liked best. I visited LSU, Kansas, and Vanderbilt before I went to Arkansas.

"After hanging with the guys at Arkansas, I knew I liked it there. I was on my way to visit with coach [Danny] Ford when Jim Washburn, the defensive line coach, saw me and called me into his office. He told me Arkansas needed me. He said they had a lot of the other ingredients to win but needed a quarterback. Since it came from a defensive line coach who wasn't even the one recruiting me, I was impressed.

"When I sat down with Coach Ford he told me the quarterback situation. Pete Burks was the only one coming back. I never make spur-of-the-moment decisions, but I told him this is where I wanted to come. He told me to slow down because he wanted to make sure this is what I wanted to do. I had considered LSU, but when I went to a basketball game on my visit to Arkansas and saw the support the school had, I knew Arkansas is where I wanted to go to school."

From the moment he stepped on campus, Stoerner was already the No. 2 quarterback. Burks was a little-used sophomore, who had played behind Barry Lunney Jr., the previous season. Stoerner played sparingly, but by the spring of his freshman year it was obvious he would move ahead of Burks.

"The only thing that concerned me at that time was when Coach Ford considered hiring Chuck Reedy as his offensive coordinator," Stoerner says. "The Baytown quarterback before me went to Baylor where Reedy was running the option. He was stuck in the wrong system. We had run some option at Arkansas, and it was all new to me. If that became our main offense, I was going to transfer.

"But they hired Kay Stephenson as offensive coordinator and Joe Ferguson as quarterbacks coach. Everything fell into place for me. Joe was the best coach I've ever had. He is a hard worker. I never stepped on the field unprepared. We went to a pro-style offense out of the option. By the end of the year we were pretty good at it. I thought if we stuck with it we could be pretty good the next year."

However, Ford was fired after the 1997 season, and the Razorbacks hired Houston Nutt as head coach. At first Stoerner didn't know what to think. He was thrilled that Nutt at least retained Ferguson.

"Coach Ford was an old-school coach," Stoerner says. "Our team had been beaten down. I'm not saying that is the wrong way to do it, because Coach Ford was a very successful coach, but we didn't know how to take Coach Nutt. I knew our team had talent and figured there was no way we could go anywhere but up, but Coach Nutt came in talking about having fun every day when before we had been doing things out of fear.

"We weren't sure it would be real, but in the offseason Coach Nutt changed so many guys' outlook on football and our team came together. We were grateful for the drastic change. Football was fun again."

Football became extremely fun in 1998 as the Razorbacks startled the SEC by starting 8-0.

"After we were about 4-0, we realized we were good," Stoerner recalls. "We knew we had to play hard to win. We couldn't take anything for granted. But we had a good football team. We thought we could beat anyone."

The bubble burst somewhat with a crushing defeat at Tennessee and then a one-point loss at Mississippi State, but the Razorbacks rebounded with a victory over LSU that earned them a spot in the Florida Citrus Bowl.

THE SEASON

Arkansas's sudden success under Nutt revived hope in the state. Plans were made to enlarge Razorback Stadium, and with so many starters returning, the Hogs were picked to win the SEC Western Division title.

"We had come within two plays of having the chance to play for the national championship in 1998," Stoerner says. "At that point we believed Coach Nutt's hype and thought anything was possible. All our receivers were back. We had a lot of things to live up to."

The Hogs started with a win over SMU and were leading Louisiana–Monroe in the fourth quarter when Stoerner suffered an injury.

"It was a fluke," Stoerner says. "Our offense was backed up, and our back-up quarterback had struggled when he went in earlier. Coach Nutt told me to take one more series. He wanted me to get us out of the hole. On a third-down pass I got hit and a guy laid on me. I hurt my shoulder.

"A lot was made of that, but it wasn't hurt bad. It really didn't bother me the rest of the year in a game, but I missed every practice before we played Alabama and wasn't sharp in that game. I was wild. We should have beaten Alabama but lost by a touchdown."

The following week Stoerner suffered his second lowest point as an Arkansas quarterback. He was benched during the Hogs' loss at Kentucky.

"Kentucky jumped on us, and we could never catch up," Stoerner recalls. "Coach Nutt had gotten flak for playing me at Alabama after I hadn't practiced. Getting pulled was hard to swallow, but I can understand why it happened."

Stoerner returned to his No. 1 spot the following week, and Arkansas earned victories over Middle Tennessee, South Carolina, and Auburn before stumbling at Ole Miss. Picked to win the West, Arkansas was just 5-3 heading into the Tennessee game.

THE SCENE

In 1998 Arkansas had been 8-0 and had led No. 1-ranked Tennessee 24-22 late in the fourth quarter at Knoxville. After stopping the Vols on downs, Arkansas had been forced to kill less than two minutes if it wanted to earn its most shocking victory of its Cinderella season.

However, Stoerner had tripped over offensive lineman Brandon Burlsworth's foot and dropped the football. Tennessee recovered and drove to the winning touchdown. The Vols won 28-24, and Stoerner had never experienced a more miserable moment.

With the Volunteers ranked second nationally and coming to Fayetteville the next season, Stoerner was forced to relive the terrible memories. Stoerner was the player every media member wanted to interview. Just as he answered every question in a dejected dressing room following the 1998 game, Stoerner handled every request.

"It was intense all week," Stoerner says. "I wanted to say the right things. I told about 90 percent of what I was feeling that week and held back the other 10 percent. I never wanted to win a game more than that one. I pushed myself in practice. I wanted to be perfect. I thought I had to be Superman and hit every throw. I was willing to do whatever it took to get it done."

Razorback fans couldn't wait for the sequel. Razorback Stadium was absolutely packed when the Hogs and Vols took the field on a gorgeous November afternoon.

Clint Stoerner

THE GAME
by Clint Stoerner

I knew during the warmups I was overhyped. On the first series I was so pumped up I missed Anthony Lucas low because I was trying to be too perfect. When I looked at those Tennessee helmets, it brought back my worst memories ever.

It was hard because I'm not usually very emotional, but I was on that day. I tried to hold it all back. There are always 10 guys in the huddle looking at you. They can't do anything if the quarterback doesn't. These guys knew me in the huddle. I didn't want to do anything that would make things seem different.

Also, I never got into the crowd and all that. The quarterback has to tune all that out. But I remember how loud it was. It felt like we had 55,000 people behind us.

The first time Tennessee had the ball, their quarterback, Tee Martin, threw the ball right into the hands of David Barrett, our cornerback. David ran it back 43 yards for a touchdown. Getting ahead early relaxed us all a little bit.

During my years at Arkansas, Tennessee couldn't stop us. We stopped ourselves at times, but they rarely stopped us. There was something about Tennessee that we always played well against them. I knew if we got the ball to the key guys we would win the game.

Tennessee wasn't rattled by the early touchdown. They came back to take a 10-7 lead. That didn't make us any less confident. We put together a good long drive for a touchdown to take the lead back.

On that drive I remember hitting Lucas on the sideline for a big play. Then Joe Dean Davenport was wide open in the end zone for the touchdown.

We lost some momentum when they scored a touchdown late in the second quarter. Then they scored again to make it 24-14.

We were down by 10 points but we had such a sense of confidence that day that we never doubted we'd win. Coach Nutt was never down. There was no panic on the sidelines. We knew they'd make us beat them by passing the ball, and we were confident we could do that.

Late in the third quarter Boo Williams got behind their defense. He made a great catch and scored a touchdown. That put us within three points. In practice Boo Williams was an All-American. During the 1999 season we focused so much on Lucas that we didn't use Boo enough. Coach Nutt called a deep route, because he knew they would be in one-on-one coverage. Boo made a big play. He got behind them and stretched to get into the end zone. That got the crowd in it again. Then we knew we would win.

Midway through the fourth quarter we made our final push. We mixed the running and passing game. We threw a pass to Emanuel Smith on the first play of the drive and then used the running game. Cedric Cobbs, Chrys Chukwuma, and Michael Jenkins each carried the ball on the next five plays, and we advanced to the Tennessee 23.

Then I did something I never would have done until my senior year. Coach Nutt sent in a play from the sidelines, but I changed it in the huddle. I knew the call would work. On the first play of the drive I remember seeing the safety come down on the pass to Smith. Coach Nutt sent in a play called X7 Bend Double Post. It's a safe play with Lucas being the No. 1 receiver on the sideline. Remembering the safety had been coming down, I left the X7 Bend off and called a Double Post. If it didn't work I could always tell Coach Nutt I didn't see the X7 Bend part when he signaled it from the sidelines.

It was a play action pass. I had my back to the line. When I turned around, I made a short pump inside to Smith. Sure enough, the safety bit. Lucas had his guy beat, but there wasn't much field to work with, so I had to throw the ball more on a line. I knew if I put it out there anywhere close to him, Lucas would get it. Sure enough, he did.

The year before I felt like I let my teammates, our fans, and the entire state of Arkansas down. At the point of Lucas's catch I felt the exact opposite. There was a weight lifted from me. I felt we had lifted a weight off the whole state.

The game wasn't over, though. Martin was a national championship quarterback the year before. He took his team down the field like you would expect him to.

Kenoy Kennedy, Barrett, and all of our defensive players never flinched, even when Tennessee moved inside our 20. Tennessee was close, but we knew they wouldn't score.

A year after suffering the heartbreak of a last-minute fumble, I took the snap, then took a knee, and watched the clock expire. The scoreboard said Arkansas 28, Tennessee 24. I was very aware it was the same score they beat us by the previous year at Knoxville.

It was special to take a knee and end the game. All my emotions came out. They are still with me today. We stayed on the field an hour after the game signing autographs and shaking hands. I broke down a couple times.

POSTGAME

The following week Arkansas beat 11th-ranked Mississippi State 14-9 at Little Rock to secure a bid to the Cotton Bowl. The Hogs were matched with old Southwest Conference rival Texas in Stoerner's last game.

"You could tell it was special to play Texas," Stoerner says. "None of us had been around for the glory days of the Arkansas–Texas rivalry, but coach [Frank] Broyles came into our team meetings to tell us how important the game was. Even if the players didn't understand the significance at first, we did once we heard from Coach Broyles."

Broyles coached the Razorbacks 19 years before becoming full-time athletic director, and some of his greatest triumphs and tragedies came against Texas.

"We felt we owed the state a great game for all the fans had done for us," Stoerner says. "It was a great way to finish my career."

Arkansas beat Texas 27-6 with Stoerner having a terrific second half. It was the 17th victory in two years directed by Stoerner, and the Hogs finished in the top 20 for the second consecutive season.

WHAT HAPPENED TO CLINT STOERNER?

S toerner signed as a free agent and spent three years with the Dallas Cowboys before playing briefly with the Miami Dolphins. He also spent two summers playing football in Europe.

He started a business in northwest Arkansas while continuing to pursue his dream of playing football. He still quarterbacks Dallas's team in the Arena Football League and passed for 77 touchdowns in 2005.

"I grew up a lot from the 1998 Tennessee game," Stoerner says. "I learned a lot about myself. I can talk about it now. To go from the 1998 game to winning the 1999 game by the same score was unbelievable.

"It's funny. When people see me now they always want to talk about my career. Even after we beat Tennessee and Texas in 1999, they still bring up the 1998 Tennessee game. I guess I can understand it. I'll always remember that game, but I'm glad we came back and won the next year."

CHAPTER 24

BRAD TAYLOR

Born: November 2, 1962
Hometown: Danville
Current Residence: Danville
Occupation: Public Relations, Chambers Bank
Position: Quarterback
Height: 6-0
Weight: 185
Years Lettered: 1981-1984
Accomplishments: Finished his career as Arkansas all-time passing leader with 4,802 yards, a total that still ranks fourth best by a Razorback; completed 333 of his 644 passes with 23 tosses for touchdowns; is currently fifth on Arkansas's career total offense list with 5,145 yards, a record when he graduated.
The Game: Arkansas vs. Baylor, November 7, 1981, at Little Rock, Arkansas

BACKGROUND

B rad Taylor had never lifted weights until he enrolled at the University of Arkansas. He didn't have to. Growing up on a farm in the Danville area, he built natural strength handling daily chores.

"On the farm I did everything," Taylor says. "I bailed hay, fed cows, and did all of the things you do on a farm. Every day was a good workout. Dad made sure I was always working. I didn't mind. I still do it today.

"In fact, I'm still doing a lot of the same things today like wrecking vehicles and tearing up stuff. Nothing ever gets broken if you never do anything. The farm life isn't for everyone. Jay Bequette, the center at Arkansas my first two years there, wouldn't have a clue what to do on a farm.

"When you lift feed sacks, it's a lot like doing squats and bench presses. When it's 100 degrees and you have 1,500 bales of hay to haul, you can't help getting a good workout. That's why we farm boys are strong and thick headed."

No matter how many hours Taylor worked, he always had time for sports.

"I started playing before I could walk," he recalls. "I played everything. I would have played hockey if we had it.

"I remember coming home from grade school and my clothes were ripped from playing football on the playground. We weren't allowed to play tackle, so defenders would grab my shirt and rip the buttons off.

"I loved playing baseball and basketball, too. Baseball was probably my best sport. I pitched and played shortstop. I wanted to play at Arkansas, but coach [Lou] Holtz wouldn't let me, especially after I started some as a freshman."

Taylor was one of Arkansas's easiest recruits to sign.

"Danville only had 1,700 people," Taylor explains. "I'm guessing not a lot of schools knew about me. Ken Turner recruited me for Arkansas. I told him not to worry. I wasn't going anywhere else. I didn't even take many other calls.

"I'd like to see that return to Arkansas today. If a young man grows up in Arkansas, he shouldn't go anywhere else to play football."

THE SEASON

T aylor wanted to be a Razorback so badly that he was never disillusioned when there were several quarterbacks on campus when he arrived in the fall of 1981.

"We had at least four other quarterbacks, and they all had talent," he says. "So, for the first four weeks I was there I was a defensive back and a wide receiver.

"One day in practice Coach Holtz saw me throwing against the starting defense. I was completing some passes. At that point I didn't really care where I played. When you have Billy Ray Smith and Richard Richardson chasing you while you are trying to pass, you don't mind playing another position."

From the moment Taylor arrived on campus he knew the Hogs would be good. Smith was an Outland Trophy candidate, and the entire Razorback defense was loaded with veterans. The offensive line was solid, and Gary Anderson led a strong group of running backs. Tom Jones was a returning starter at quarterback.

"I was the No. 3 quarterback behind Tom and Bill Pierce," Jones says. "I hardly played until they put me in late against Texas. We were already ahead 39-3. It was great being part of that game, but I didn't do much."

Texas was ranked No. 1 in the country when the Razorbacks drilled the Longhorns 42-11 at Fayetteville. Arkansas was 5-1 after that win and led Houston 14-0 the following week when Jones went down with an injury. Pierce played most of the rest of the game with Taylor coming in late. The Razorbacks ended up losing 20-17.

"I was scared to death but excited, too, when they put me in against Houston. Coach Holtz told me whatever I did not to throw an interception. We ran a deep route on my first pass, and I threw the ball 80 yards. It was way overthrown, but I got an ovation for a pass that went 80 yards."

The following Monday Taylor was tabbed to start against Rice. He was more than ready by game day.

"Coach Holtz hammered me with everything to get me prepared," Taylor says. "After every practice Larry Beightol, our offensive line coach, went over checks with me. They simplified things somewhat, so I wouldn't be worn out.

"I remember calling home that week to tell my parents I was starting. It was a pretty big deal in Danville for one of their own to be the starting quarterback at the University of Arkansas."

It poured rain in Houston, but Taylor played so well against the Owls that he was named Southwest Conference Player of the Week. Arkansas won 41-7 to improve to 6-2.

THE SCENE

The next week the Razorbacks faced Baylor in Little Rock and Taylor was still tagged as the starter.

"Even though I had started the week before, I was no more comfortable getting ready for Baylor. They were always physical. They'd beat you to death. I was so focused on learning that Saturday got here before I knew it.

"It was my first in-state start. It was a really big to run through that 'A' at Little Rock and hear the fans holler. I think everyone that lived in Danville was there. I didn't want to disappoint those fans from Danville. A lot of people said no one from a town that small could play at a school like Arkansas. I wanted to make our community proud."

Brad Taylor

THE GAME
by Brad Taylor

It was a great offensive game. They'd score just as fast as we would. There was no time to sit around and think about things. We always had to do something on offense.

Honestly I thought we could score every time we had the ball. We stopped ourselves some. Baylor's defense was physical, but we were very prepared for them. This is terrible to admit—the game has been so long ago I probably can admit it now—but there were times I thought maybe they'll score so we can get back on the field. We were that confident on offense.

Gary Anderson and Jessie Clark were great backs, and they were incredible that night. I got in trouble for watching those guys run instead of carrying out my fakes. I'd hand the ball off and watch them. They were unreal. I didn't want to miss seeing them run.

Baylor was physical. They would tear your head off. Jessie Clark got beat up that night, but he played well. He scored five touchdowns, and I watched all of them.

Even when we got behind I was never nervous. I scrambled a lot and hit some second and third receivers. We kept scoring, but they did, too. We were having a great time on offense. Coach Holtz told me later my peripheral vision that night was the best he had ever seen.

We scored the first touchdown, but by the end of the first quarter we were behind 17-10. Both teams scored a touchdown in the second quarter, so it was 24-17 at the half. But like I said earlier, we were never worried. We knew we could score.

Baylor even went ahead by 10 points in the third quarter, but we scored on three straight possessions to build an 11-point lead. Jessie scored all three touchdowns. He was unstoppable that night, but he was running behind a great line. Jay Bequette, Steve Korte, Alfred Mohammed, and the others took care of me and blocked for Jessie and Gary.

Even when we were ahead by 11 points, we never felt comfortable. We were glad to be ahead, but we knew we would have to score again.

Sure enough, Baylor came back to take the lead. They went for two after scoring their last touchdown, but we stopped them. That was really big. We were only trailing by a point and just needed a field goal.

We got the ball back with about two minutes left. We were confident we'd score but were conscious of using the clock, too. I remember scrambling and hitting Mark Mistler on a third-down play. Darryl Mason made a big catch on that drive, too.

It was remarkable Darryl was in the game. Earlier I hung him out to dry on a pass over the middle. Van McElroy was Baylor's free safety, and he was one of the fiercest hitters to ever play the game. I saw Darryl come open, but when I let the ball go, I saw McElroy coming. I thought, "Oh no!"

Darryl made the catch just before McElroy hit him. The hit knocked Darryl's teeth out. I felt terrible. I wanted to apologize to him, but he came back to the huddle spitting teeth out.

"Good pass," he said.

"Good catch."

What else could I say after a play like that?

Anyway, he made a big catch on our last drive, and we moved the ball to within field-goal range. Bruce Lahay, our kicker, was automatic when he was in his range. He didn't have a real strong leg, but if the ball was in his zone, it was good. We moved plenty close. He was a senior, but Greg Garrison, our snapper, and I were freshmen. I held for extra points and field goals that year.

Greg snapped it perfectly, I held, and Bruce drilled it. There were only seven seconds left, so Baylor had no way of coming back.

It was a great win, but I remember feeling relieved. I didn't let the team or the people of Danville down. I was relaxed and had fun. I knew what to do in every situation. That's how well prepared I was. Lou Holtz was on me all the time, but he believed in me and thought I could do the job.

POSTGAME

After the exhilaration of the 41-39 victory over Baylor in which Taylor completed 17 of his 23 passes for 250 yards, the Hogs edged Texas A&M 10-7 the following week at College Station. In a Friday interview Taylor told ABC-TV's Keith Jackson that there wasn't anything nearly as big as Texas A&M's football stadium in Danville and mentioned the population of Danville wouldn't even fill a section at A&M.

The Hogs earned a spot in the Gator Bowl against North Carolina, but Taylor didn't get to enjoy the activities. He was too busy preparing for the game.

"It was the first bowl game for me," he says. "I was drilled and drilled. Everyone else was having fun, but I had to study. It was a unique experience. The fog was so thick you could hardly see. My first three or four passes went into the third row. Coach Holtz told me to calm down, and I was okay after that. Neither team could stop the other, and North Carolina scored more than we did."

After starting for most of the final half of the 1981 season, Taylor split time with Tom Jones, who was healthy again, in 1982. The Razorbacks had a terrific season.

"It was tough for me," Taylor admits. "They sent me in on third and 15 or third and 20. I threw the ball a bunch, but the defensive backs knew what was coming.

"I learned a lot from Tom that year. He didn't have extraordinary ability, but he would beat you with his brain."

Arkansas finished 9-2-1 and graduated one of the greatest senior classes in school history. Taylor was the clear-cut starter in 1983, but it was a much younger team. The Hogs were 6-5, and Holtz was fired after the season.

"Coach Holtz was hard on me, but he took care of me. He was my biggest cheerleader on the sideline. It hurt when we found out he was leaving. I felt bad about the way it happened, but there was nothing I could do.

"I still have great respect for Coach Holtz. I visited with him one year in Little Rock when he was coaching South Carolina. He remembered things like they happened yesterday. Football gives you a special bond. I had that bond with two different groups at Arkansas.

"I bonded with the seniors of 1982, because I started as a freshman. I lived with Billy Ray Smith one summer. I had to be one of the few that had to stir Steve Korte's ice cream, because I was a freshman but also got welcomed because I started."

Korte convinced Taylor to do more than stir his ice cream. It was the prompting of the offensive guard that motivated Taylor to do something no other UA quarterback had done before or has since.

"Someone told Korte I could throw the ball 100 yards, so he told me to do it," Taylor says. "I figured if Steve Korte told you to do something, you did it. It was the first time I had ever tried to throw the ball 100 yards. I did it but didn't think it was a big deal. When Coach Holtz found out I did it, he chewed me out and told me not to risk hurting my arm by doing that again."

Taylor didn't figure to throw any 100-yard passes when Ken Hatfield was named new head coach of the Razorbacks. Hatfield brought the Wishbone to Arkansas.

"Coach Hatfield tried to recruit me to Air Force when I was a senior in high school," Taylor says. "I told him I was going to Arkansas. I didn't know what to expect. I didn't have much experience running the option. I had read the option some in high school, but that was it.

"I was the quarterback, though. I dropped some weight so I could run. It was a learning experience. I did all right. We still threw quite a bit. We had some great come-from-behind wins and almost made it to the Cotton Bowl."

Only a narrow defeat at SMU in the season finale prevented the Hogs from sharing the SWC crown and hosting the Cotton Bowl. Instead Arkansas faced Auburn and Bo Jackson in the Liberty Bowl.

"After the Liberty Bowl I couldn't believe my career was over," Taylor says. "There was no practice the next day. It was hard to say goodbye to my teammates. When you go to battle with someone, you really have something special."

WHAT HAPPENED TO BRAD TAYLOR?

Taylor played three years in the Canadian Football League after his Razorback career had been completed. After undergoing knee surgery he returned to Danville and life on the farm.

"I love life on the farm," Taylor says. "I wouldn't do anything else. We have cows, chickens, and pigs. I also do some public relations work at Chambers Bank. I'm as happy as a man can be."

Taylor and his wife, Kim, have a 10-year-old daughter, Tori. He keeps his football interest alive by coaching quarterbacks at Danville High School on a volunteer basis.